Copenhagen

written and researched by

LONE MOURITSEN
AND ROGER NORUM

Contents

INTRODUCTION TO

Copenhagen

Once a low-key underrated city, the Danish capital has recently been showered with superlatives. First a survey rated its citizens as the happiest on the planet. Then in 2010 local restaurant *Noma* was declared the world's best place to eat – a feat it has repeated almost every year since. More recently the city was voted as best in the world for quality of life, followed by accolades for its metro, cycling and design. Meanwhile Danish TV exports, *The Killing*, *Borgen* and *The Bridge* have brought its Nordic style, gritty architecture and photogenic inhabitants into millions of living rooms. While all this cool contentment doesn't come cheap (for tourists and locals alike) the "great Dane" has now arrived as one of Europe's outstanding destinations.

AMAGERTORV

Best places to explore on two wheels

Cycling is a way of life in Copenhagen – nearly everyone gets to school and work on two wheels. Pick up a snazzy bike for rent at Københavns Cyklebørs in Indre By, then pedal around Christianshavn's quiet canals, up to Kastellet to see the Little Mermaid or out to Frederiksberg's lush parks. Alternatively, hop on a train (bike in tow) up the coast, then pedal out to see the world-class art of the Louisiana Museum or around Kronborg Castle, one of the most handsome fortresses in the land.

Part of Copenhagen's appeal is its hybrid nature, a unique blend of mainland Europe and Scandinavia. The city looks as much to London, Berlin and Amsterdam as it does to Stockholm or Oslo, perhaps a legacy of its swashbuckling seafaring and trading history. Its gregarious English-speaking inhabitants can also seem positively welcoming compared with the icy reserve of their northerly neighbours.

If the city lacks anything you could say it's a true "blockbuster" attraction. Aside from the Little Mermaid and arguably the Tivoli Gardens, Copenhagen doesn't do the "queue round the block" tourism, while its most illustrious former inhabitants (Hans Christian Andersen aside) don't quite make the global pilgrimage hit list. Instead you'll discover a marvellously eclectic range of museums, galleries, designer shops and royal heritage buildings, all easily digestible and perfect for short-break perusing. For an idea of where to begin turn to our itineraries and 'best of' sections.

Whether you're on foot, cycling (see box above) or jumping on the user-friendly transport system you'll also find Copenhagen eminently navigable. You can quickly flit between neighbourhoods, from the cobbled avenues of Frederiksstaden and grand Slotsholmen island to the winding medieval streets of the Latin Quarter and the gritty boho chic of Nørrebro. Green space and charming canals are never far away, whether in the landscaped Kongens Have, or postcard-cute Nyhavn. For those schooled in Dansk design and architecture a visit to Christianshavn will reveal the city's more adventurous

NYHAVN

When to visit

Easily Copenhagen's best season is summer, when both locals and visitors stay out nursing their drinks until the wee hours and cultural events such as the ten-day-long Copenhagen Jazz Festival bring live music, dance and art to the streets. Autumn and spring are similarly alluring – especially for cycling – since the afternoons remain warm but the majority of tourists have departed. Still, don't write off winter, a perfectly charming time for drinking *gløg* (Scandinavian mulled wine) in cosy bars and enjoying the beloved Danish tradition of *hygge* (cosiness). Tivoli's festive markets and the city's Christmas Parade make the city an excellent destination for a festive break.

side: big open skies and sleek glass and chrome modernism. Come nightfall and another Copenhagen emerges – Michelin-star chefs shout out orders, cocktails are shaken and craft beers cracked open (see opposite for the best neighbourhoods to try).

Given Denmark itself is such a small country, the capital is also but a hop, skip and a jump away from some other cracking destinations. Half an hour west is medieval Roskilde, home to a superb museum of Viking shipbuilding and also home to one of Europe's best outdoor summer music festivals. North of the capital, meanwhile, stands the outstanding modern art museum of Louisiana, the picture-perfect Renaissance castle of Kronborg and – across the iconic Øresund Bridge – the cool, diminutive Swedish city of Malmö, once part of Denmark's regal orbit.

COPENHAGEN AT A GLANCE

>> EATING

The Danish capital currently boasts a record fifteen Michelin stars – more than anywhere else in Scandinavia (see box, p.72). While advance booking at the better-known dining spots is recommended, Copenhagen isn't all haute cuisine: you can also find great local and international spots such as Christianshavn's *Bådudlejning*, *Café* and *Ølhalle* and *Pintxos* which will suit slightly slimmer purses. Furthermore, restaurants all over the city often offer affordable lunchtime options, and you can always visit Nørrebro's Torvehaller market for everything from organic wines to freshly baked goods – especially on Sundays, when many city restaurants close their doors anyway.

>> DRINKING

The Danes consume more coffee than anywhere else in the world, and to this end downtown Copenhagen is paradise for caffeine addicts – *Café Norden* and *Café Europe* are two of Indre By's most popular. Many daytime cafés often morph into cosy and candlelit bars come eveningtime, and nearly anywhere in Copenhagen you can find music lilting from inside a chilled bar until very late – perfect for enjoying a relaxing pint of Carlsberg or one of Denmark's many excellent microbrews (don't miss Ølfabriken's traditional stouts). Most recently, the city has acquired some great wine bars, most notably in Vesterbro and Nørrebro.

>> NIGHTLIFE

If you're in the market for late nights out, the trendy meatpacking district of Kødbyen should be your first – or, rather, last – stop. This recently gentrified neighbourhood of lofts and warhouses has become one of Europe's hottest places to party with DJs, live bands and plenty of dancing. For something more mellow, try Sankt Hans Torv and the surrounding streets in Nørrebro, probably the best place in the city for a romantic late-night drink. Don't miss a shot of ice-cold caraway schnapps – a Danish speciality.

>> SHOPPING

To get your retail kicks, the central cobbled pedestrian Strøget offers large department stores, including Illums Bolighus, a favourite with the Danish queen, plus iconic local brands Royal Copenhagen and Georg Jensen. The nearby streets of Købmagergade and Kompagnistræde have small, independent holes-in-the-wall selling modern design *objets* and housewares, while the student-filled Latin Quarter is the place to head for secondhand fashion. South, Værnedamsvej in Vesterbro is great for local designers, while northerly Nørrebro (especially Elmegade and Krystalgade) offers chic shops with designers on hand to tailor the clothing on the racks to fit you perfectly.

OUR RECOMMENDATIONS FOR WHERE TO EAT, DRINK AND SHOP ARE LISTED AT THE END OF EACH CHAPTER.

Day One in Copenhagen

1 Latin Quarter, Inner City > p.39. Begin the day strolling about this maze of lively medieval streets and squares around Copenhagen University, perfect for losing yourself in history.

2 Rådhus > p.36. Climb to the tower of this grandiose, National Romantic city hall, whose fascinating astronomical clock is a destination in itself.

Lunch > *Aamanns* (see p.74). This rustic-urban eatery does modern takes on the traditional Danish smørrebrød.

3 Canal Tour > p. 131. Join one of the multilingual hourly tours along Copenhagen's centuries-old canals, which offer fascinating insight into important events and sights tied to Denmark's tumultuous history.

4 Rosenborg Slot > p. 68. Explore your inner royal at this fairytale, red-brick Renaissance castle, whose cellar holds the Danish crown jewels and Frederik III's coronation throne, made of gold and narwhal tusk.

5 Nyboder > p. 73. Make your way out to the multi-coloured terraced houses in this relaxed part of town, built in the 17th century to house the Danish navy.

Dinner > *Tolboden* (see p.67). This spacious, casual restaurant is set opposite the royal yacht's mooring and is unbeatable for people-watching.

6 The Little Mermaid > p. 63. Stroll out to Kastellet to catch a glimpse of Copenhagen's mascot and the heroine of Hans Christian Andersen's fairytale.

Day Two in Copenhagen

1 Ny Carlsberg Glyptotek > p.34. Start off in this brilliant museum, which holds a vast classical and modern European art collection displayed in opulent rooms.

2 Danish Design Centre > p.35. This Henning Larsen-designed, glass-fronted museum-cum-shop has a permanent collection of Zippo lighters, Wonderbras and other design classics.

3 Christiania > p.80. Amble along the pretty Christianshavns Kanal, designed by an Amsterdam-born architect, before exploring this renowned hippie "free city" commune.

Lunch > *Cofoco* (see p.92). This popular spot's scrumptious fresh dishes hail straight from the island of Bornholm in the middle of the Baltic Sea.

4 Frederiksberg Have > p.90. Pedal out towards Værnedamsvej for a spot of fashionista window shopping, then put down on the open expanses of grass at the city's most wild parklands.

5 Københavns Museum > p.88. Scale models and antique photographs tell the history of the capital, while a small room upstairs fills you in on local philosopher Søren Kierkegaard.

6 Helsingør > p.109. Ride the train up the coast to watch the sun set against Kronborg, a fairytale fortress and the inspiration for Elsinore Castle in Shakespeare's Hamlet.

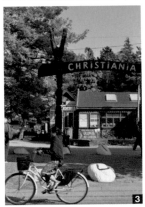

Dinner > *Brasserie Nimb* (see p.37). Great traditional French food with a regularly changing menu in an Oriental-style palace, with views out to Tivoli Gardens.

Kids Copenhagen

Families will find plenty to keep the kids happy from amusement parks to swimming pools, science museums to playgrounds.

1 Tivoli > p.32. This magical fairground has roller coasters, pantomime theatres and endless helpings of family fun.

2 Havneparken > p.82. Visit the sandy city beach "Copencabana", popular with children thanks to its two outdoor pools and diving boards built right into the harbour.

3 Rundetårn > p.39. This 42m-high stone church tower has an observatory at the top offering great vistas across to the city's numerous spires.

Lunch > Søren K (p.57). Casual food for kids (and champagne and oysters for parents) served up in a wonderful setting.

4 Tøjhusmuseet > p.56. Young boys will adore Denmark's national arsenal museum, filled with swords, firearms, cannons and umpteen warfare accoutrements.

5 Ridebane > p.54. Girls will love the Royal Riding Grounds, whose regal, marble-clad stables are home to golden carriages and beautiful horses.

6 Experimentarium > p.99. This huge science lab lets kids learn about the human body, physics and the natural world, all with hands-on high-energy exhibits.

Dinner > Madklubben (see p.66). This much-loved Danish chain offers delicious meals at surprisingly affordable prices.

Budget Copenhagen

Though Copenhagen is Europe's third most expensive capital, you can save cash by using a discount card, riding free city bikes, taking harbour bus-boats and visiting many of the city's free-entry museums.

1 National Museum > p.36. Home to Denmark's finest ethnographic artefacts, including an extensive collection of Viking weapons and coins.

2 Amalienborg > p.60. A few metres from the harbourfront, soldiers participate in the Changing of the Guard here at noon every day.

Lunch > Pick up some bread, cheese and drinks, then picnic on the grass of Kongens Have (see p.69), the city's most popular green space.

3 Marmorkirken > p.61. This marble church was built in 1894 in the image of St Peter's in Rome; join the 1pm tour to ascend the 260 steps to the dome's apogee for some grand city views.

4 Slotsholmen > p.52. Descend a narrow stairwell to explore the ruins of two excavated underground castles.

5 Assistens Kirkegaard > p.96. Cross the western lakes to take in the final resting place of Danish luminaries such as Hans Christian Andersen and Niels Bohr.

6 Galerie Asbæk > p.64. This much-loved gallery represents some of Denmark's best-known painters and photographers and is great for a spot of window shopping.

Dinner > *Vespa* (see p.67). This simple, down-at-heel Italian restaurant's four-course set menus are outstanding value for money.

.ism is both
.g. > **p.57**

Architecture

1 The Black Diamond This stunning piece of waterfront modern
a concert hall and a super spot for picnicking and people-watchin

2 Marmorkirken Taking 145 years to complete, this grandiose marble church has a specatular bell tower, reached by climbing 260 tortuous steps. **> p.61**

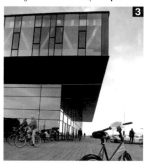

3 Skuespilhuset This sleek extension to the Danish Royal Theatre is a wonderful spot for lunch. **> p.61**

4 Rundetårn Christian IV's 40m tower, accessed by a unique spiral walkway, provides one of the best vantage points over the city. **> p.39**

5 Carlsberg Byen The historic Carslberg quarter is full of quirky architecural features including the wonderful Elephant Gate. **> p.89**

Eating

1 Laundromat Wonderful little café that doubles as a launderette. Brilliant burgers and fries, which you can linger over while playing backgammon. **> p.102**

2 Madklubben You don't have to be mad to eat here – delicious, affordable food from this popular Danish chain (branches in Tivoli and Vesterbro). **> p.66**

3 Noma Regularly topping the list of the world's greatest restaurants, *Noma* has retained its inventiveness and ability to surprise. **> p.84**

4 Aamanns Stylish restaurant that has reinvented the Danish smørrebrød (open sandwich), with fresh, innovative ingredients. **> p.74**

5 La Glace You haven't tried a true Danish pastry until you've visited this Copenhagen icon, open since 1870. Also does legendary ice cream. **> p.46**

Art

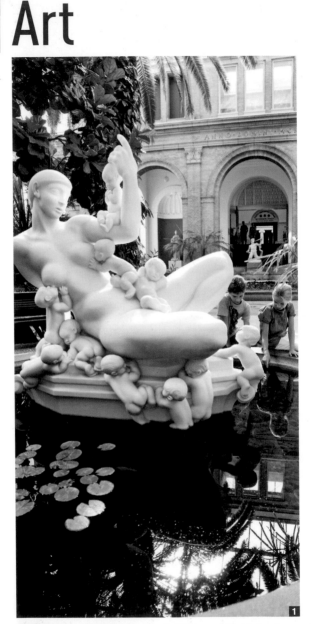

1 Ny Carlsberg Glyptotek From Classical Roman sculptures to French impressionists, some of Europe's most enviable art resides at this glass-domed, palm-filled museum. **> p.34**

2 Hirschsprungske Samling A wonderfully intimate gallery showcasing Danish masterpieces from the collection of Heinrich Hirschsprung. **> p.71**

4 Christiania The "free city" showcases evocative street art painted on its ramparts, walls and shacks – well worth an exploration. **> p.80**

3 Statens Museum for Kunst Denmark's national gallery provides everything from Italian religious art to Picasso and Matisse. **> p.70**

5 Louisiana Amble away a day in the twisting corridors of this unique museum, known for its Giacomettis, Rodchenkos and Warhols. **> p.108**

Shopping

1 Strøget Big department stores rub shoulders with small independent boutiques along the world's longest pedestrianized street. **> p.38**

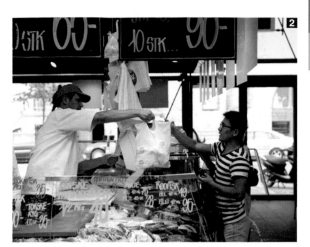

2 Torvehallerne An atmospheric covered food market purveying upscale Danish delicacies and prime produce. > **p.73**

3 Royal Copenhagen Head to the porcelain giant's flagship store for stylish gifts and kitchenware. > **p.45**

4 Ecouture by Lund Unique and environmentally conscious fashion created by local costume designer Johanne Helger Lund. > **p.99**

5 Paustian High-end designer furniture and more affordable accessories sold in a beautifully designed building. > **p.100**

Waterfront

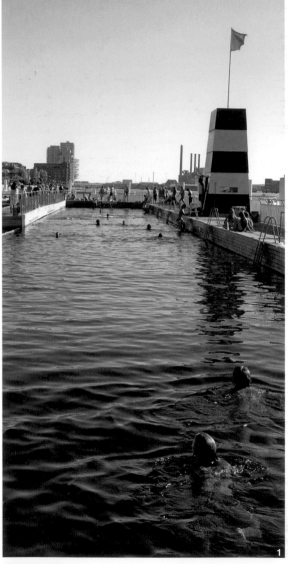

1 Havneparken Brace yourself for a dip in the Harbour Park pool, a favourite hangout in summer (and open on New Year's Day should you fancy it). **> p.82**

2 **Nyhavn** This quaint much-photographed harbour is located just alongside a strip of popular bars and restaurants. **> p.58**

3 **Christianshavns Kanal** Stroll (or kayak) about one of Copenhagen's most quiet, handsome canals, right in the heart of the city. **> p.78**

4 **Amager Strandpark** Just south of the city, this clean sandy beach has views of the Øresund bridge. **> p.110**

5 **Halvandet** Urban beach bar that's a favourite with the beautiful people, who come for the laid-back beats and cool, Ibiza-esque vibe. **> p.85**

Drinking

1 **Alfresco bars** Summer or winter, Danes have perfected the art of outdoor drinking – try Vesterbro and Nørrebro for the best in streetside idling. **> p.94 & 104**

2 Kødbyen Copenhagen's meatpacking district is the hippest area for a night out. **> p.88**

3 Øl Baren Serving literally hundreds of different European beers, this Vesterbro institution is a must for beer geeks. **> p.105**

4 Oak Room Swinging little joint serving fabulous cocktails including the Slutty Mary, a tequila-infused Bloody Mary with lime, coriander and chilli. **> p.105**

5 Mikkeller An elegant, modernist pub appealing both to craft ale hipsters and design fans thanks to its beautifully constructed interior. **> p.95**

Museums

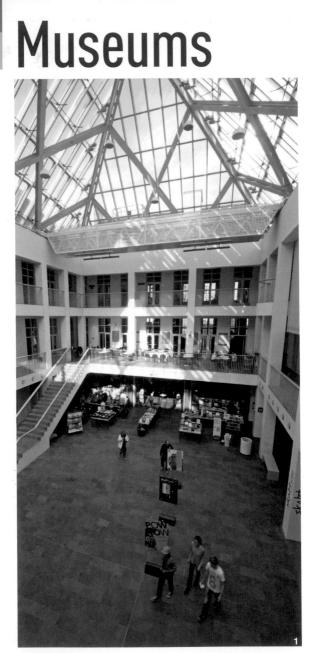

1 National Museum World-class collection of historical artefacts, from bog people and fifteenth-century BC sculptures to Viking weapons. **> p.36**

2 Thorvaldsens Museum Copenhage n-born Bertel Thorvaldsen was one of Europe's finest Neoclassical sculptors. Here you'll find his greatest works including Jason with the Golden Fleece. **> p.55**

3 Experimentarium This massive science centre will keep the kids entertained for hours. **> p.99**

4 Designmuseum Denmark Trace the evolution of Danish design from Renaissance textiles to Arne Jacobsen chairs – Ikea it ain't. **> p.62**

5 Blue Planet Opened in March 2013, this jaw-dropping modern aquarium holds some 20,000 animals across 450 species. **> p.110**

Royalty

1 Guards at the Amalienborg Kids love the royal palace's poker-faced guards, who ceremoniously change their position every day at noon. > **p.60**

2 Frederiksborg Fairytale renaissance castle spread out across several small islands, featuring a lake, gardens, Gothic towers and spires. **> p.109**

3 Crown jewels Swords, sceptres and gilded crowns, kept safe in the the Rosenborg Slot **> p.68**

4 Reception Rooms Tapestries Bjørn Nørgaard's technicolour modern tapestries are hung high in the Great Hall, showcasing the history of Denmark. **> p.52**

5 Royal stables Coaches, carriages and around twenty particularly well-groomed steeds. **> p.54**

PLACES

Tivoli and Rådhuspladsen

Tivoli, Denmark's most-visited attraction, may appear at first glance every bit as tacky as any other amusement park around the world, but it has much more to offer than just its thrilling set of rides. After taking in the 83,000-square-metre gardens, with their gorgeous flower displays and fountains, romantic boating lake, exotic-looking buildings (from Chinese pagodas to Moorish palaces) and – at night – spectacular illuminations, even the most cynical visitor will have to succumb and agree that it's a magical (albeit expensive) place. A few paces away is the buzzing Rådhuspladsen square, towered over by the grand red-brick nineteenth-century city hall, whose innards hold a fascinating astronomical clock. As well as demarcating the city's geographical heart, the square is the perfect place for a mustard-topped *pølse*.

TIVOLI

Vesterbrogade 3 ☎ 33 15 10 01, ✺ tivoli.dk. Mid-April to mid-Sept, two weeks in Oct & mid-Nov to Dec Mon–Thurs & Sun 11am–10pm, Fri 11am–0.30am, Sat 11am–midnight. Adults and children aged 8 and over 95kr; under 8s free. Rides 25–75kr, multi-ride pass 199kr. MAP OPPOSITE, POCKET MAP A13

Opened in 1843, **Tivoli** was the creation of architect George Carstensen, who had been commissioned by King Christian VIII to build a pleasure garden for the masses outside the western gate into the city. It was an immediate success, and – expanded and modernized over the years – was a major influence on Walt Disney for his theme parks a century later. That the gardens continue even today to occupy such a patch of prime real

TIVOLI

ACCOMMODATION	
Cab-Inn City	7
Danhostel City	6
Hotel Nimb	5
Hotel Twentyseven	3
Palace Hotel	1
Radisson Blu Royal Hotel	4
The Square	2

CAFÉS AND RESTAURANTS	
Brasserie Nimb	5
Glyptoteket	6
Grøften	3
Kanal Cafeen	4
Madklubben	2

BAR	
Oscar Bar og Café	1

VENUE	
Mojo	1

Tivoli and Rådhuspladsen

estate, sandwiched between the Hovedbanegården and the Rådhus, is testimony to Tivoli's central place within the city's affections.

Tivoli's principal draw, of course – to children at least – is its thirty-odd **rides**, which include one of the world's oldest still-functioning wooden roller coasters. Still more hair-raising are the Spinning Top, which lifts up and twirls thrill-seekers around some 80m above ground, and the Star Flyer which thrusts its victims around at the nauseating force of 5G. Music, theatre and panto (mostly free once you're in) are a key part of Tivoli's appeal, with five stages and a several bandstands. Pantomime – in the classic Italian *commedia dell'arte* tradition – is put on throughout the year in the extraordinary Chinese-style **Peacock Theatre**, and every Friday evening in season at 10pm there's a hugely popular gig (Ⓦfredagsrock.dk) at the open-air **Plænen** stage, featuring mainly Scandinavian acts. The gardens can get crowded but the setting is magical and the atmosphere buzzing – and Tivoli's undulating layout means that you can always find a peaceful and picturesque nook from which to drink in the scene.

Formerly only open summertime, in recent years Tivoli has extended its season to include a fortnight around **Halloween**, when the gardens are bestrewn with smiley pumpkins and clingy cobwebs, and a six-week **Christmas market**, when the best of Danish Yuletide traditions are on show.

What lies beneath: digging up the town

With a brand-new orbital metro line due to open in 2017, large parts of the old city are currently under excavation, the most extensive building work since King Christian IV (aka the builder king) erected most of Copenhagen's defensive works, castles and churches in the sixteenth century. **Archeologists** at the Københavns Museum (see p.88) are having a field day (literally) unlocking the city's underground secrets before the diggers are let loose, and some aspects of its history are now under revision. New data has emerged indicating, for example, that a major settlement existed here before Bishop Absalon founded Copenhagen in the twelfth century and that the settlers at the time were much taller than previously thought. **The WALL**, an interactive mobile 12-metre screen, follows the excavators around, providing above-ground news on the latest finds and discoveries underneath. For information on where to find its consult ⓦ m.dk and ⓦ copenhagen.dk.

CENTRAL STATION

MAP P.33, POCKET MAP A14

Designed by station builder extraordinaire Heinrich Wenck as a *Gesamtkunstwerk* (total work of art), the hulking yet elegant **Hovedbanegården** (Central Station) is one of the country's most noteworthy National Romantic buildings. Dating from 1911, it's built predominantly in red brick, slate and granite, as dictated by the style, with abundant decorative detail – all of which Wenck was responsible for. Note in particular the large wood-beamed (rather than cast-iron) arches supporting the roof structure above the central hall and platforms, and the magnificent chandeliers.

The station is home to the studio of a national television channel, TV2. Journalists from the daily *Go'morgen Danmark* ("Good Morning Denmark") breakfast show often canvass opinions on the issues of the day from passing travellers so don't be surprised if you're suddenly stopped for a quick interview.

NY CARLSBERG GLYPTOTEK

Dantes Plads 7 ☎ 33 41 81 41
ⓦ glyptoteket.dk. Tues–Sun 11am–5pm, 75kr, free on Sun. Free guided tours in English June–Aug Sun 1pm (rest of the year in Danish only). MAP P.33, POCKET MAP B14

Impossible to miss with its opulent red-brick Venetian Renaissance facade, the exquisite **Ny Carlsberg Glyptotek** was established by brewing magnate Carl Jacobsen (1842–1914) to provide a public home for his vast private art collection. The

NY CARLSBERG GLYPTOTEK

building and collection have since been extended and expanded several times, the gallery's richly decorated rooms providing as captivating a spectacle as the remarkable haul of ancient and modern works on display.

The main entrance takes you into the museum's original building (1897), designed by Danish architect **Vilhelm Dahlerup**. Housed within its two floors of extravagantly colourful friezes, marble pillars and mosaic floors are sculptures and paintings from the **Danish Golden Age**, including Bertel Thorvaldsen's evocative The Three Graces relief, and a fine collection of **French sculpture**, with particular emphasis on Rodin – the largest collection of his work outside France. Undoubted highlight of the Dahlerup section however is the tranquil, glass-domed **Winter Garden** around which it centres, filled with palm trees, statues and a fountain. The museum café here serves arguably Scandinavia's best cake (see p.37).

On the opposite side of the Winter Garden, the large marble-pillared Central Hall of the elaborate **Kampmann** extension (1905) leads to an extensive **Ancient Mediterranean** collection, which starts around 6000BC and traces the development of the Greek, Etruscan and Roman empires. From the Central Hall a set of stairs leads up to newer wing designed by Henning Larsen (of the Opera House; see p.82), a courtyard infill housing a fantastic collection of **French post-impressionist** paintings including noteworthy pieces by Degas, Manet and Gauguin.

DANISH DESIGN CENTRE

H.C. Andersens Boulevard 27 ☎ 33 69 33 69, ⬤ ddc.dk. Mon, Tues, Thurs & Fri 10am–5pm, Wed 10am–9pm, Sat & Sun 11am–4pm. 55kr.
MAP P.33, POCKET MAP B13

Spread over the three floors of a glass-fronted building designed by Henning Larsen, the **Danish Design Centre** is a resource centre for cutting-edge sustainable design, both Danish and international. There's no permanent exhibition but – whatever is on – the hands-on displays and interactive screens will easily keep you occupied for a couple of hours. There's also a small café and a shop, the latter of which sells coffee-table books on contemporary design, plus a range of gadgets and gizmos.

DANISH DESIGN CENTRE

THE RÅDHUS

Rådhuspladsen ☎ 33 66 33 66. Mon–Fri
8.30am–4.30pm, Sat 10am–1pm. Access to
Jens Olsen's World Clock 10kr. Tower Mon–Fri
11am & 2pm, Sat noon; 20kr; Tours in English
Mon–Fri 3pm, Sat 10am, 30kr. MAP P.33,
POCKET MAP B13

Dominating Rådhuspladsen,
the city's bustling cobbled main
square (much of it currently
cordoned off by metro building
works), is the grand **Rådhus**
(City Hall) from 1905, a great
example of the National
Romantic style with beautiful
and intricate decorative detail
throughout. Just past the
entrance, the stately main hall
has walls of layered polished
red brick and limestone (a
reference to the national flag)
and an impressive arched
gallery, beneath which a
limestone strip is inscribed
with key moments in
Copenhagen's history. As a
working public building the
City Hall is open to visitors,
though the informative **tours**
are the best way to capture its
full detail. Tours include access
to the 105m **tower**, which gives
stunning views of the city, and
Jens Olsen's world clock – an
extraordinary astronomical
timepiece from 1955 with
hundreds of ticking dials
tracking the planetary
movement with astounding
accuracy.

NATIONALMUSEET

Ny Vestergade 10 ☎ 33 13 44 11,
Ⓦ natmus.dk. Tues–Sun 10am–5pm. Free.
MAP P.33, POCKET MAP C13

Housed in an eighteenth-
century Rococo palace, formerly
the Danish Crown Prince's
residence, the immense
National Museum's vast
collection, which stretches from
prehistory to the present day via
the Viking period and Middle
Ages, could easily take days to

NATIONAL MUSEET

go through. If you're short of
time, head straight for the
second floor and the captivating
Inuit part of the vast **Ethnographic** collection, the most
extensive of its kind in the
world. There's a wealth of detail
on their hunting techniques and
exhibits include dog sledges and
some amazing hand-carved
kayaks. It also provides a
succinct account of the events
leading to Denmark's
colonization of Greenland.
Standout among the exhibits in
the **Danish prehistory** section
are the magical gold-plated
Trundholm Sun Chariot, dating
from around 1400 BC, which
has featured on many a Danish
stamp since its discovery in
1902, and – above all – the
bog-preserved **Egtved Girl**
(1370 BC), who still has her
clothes, hair and jewellery
intact. Finally, a detour to the
Viking exhibition will
categorically banish the
perception that all Vikings did
was rape and pillage. Room 23
gives an insight into the
remarkable distances they
travelled – as far as present-day
Iran and Aghanistan – on their
trade and diplomatic missions
to gather silver, the main
currency of the era.

Cafés and restaurants

BRASSERIE NIMB

Bernstorffsgade 5 ☎ 88 70 00 10, ⓦ nimb.dk.
MAP P.33, POCKET MAP A13
One of six restaurants within the lavish *Nimb Hotel*, Tivoli's romantic fairytale *Arabian Nights*-style palace (though also accessible from outside the gardens), the ground-floor *Brasserie* is a temple to traditional French cuisine. Open throughout the year.

GLYPTOTEKET

Dantes Plads 7 ☎ 33 41 81 28,
ⓦ glyptoteket.dk. Tues–Sun 11am–5pm.
MAP P.33, POCKET MAP B14
Even if the Ny Carlsberg Glyptotek's art and sculpture don't grab you, it's worth visiting the café, occupying a beautiful position in the glass-domed Winter Garden, for exquisite smørrebrød (98kr) and cake (from 45kr).

GRØFTEN

Tivoli ☎ 33 75 06 75, ⓦ groeften.dk. See Tivoli for opening hrs. MAP P.33, POCKET MAP A13
Historic restaurant with seating outdoors on a large open terrace, popular with celebs of a certain vintage. The overloaded prawn sandwich (125kr) and the all-you-can-eat *skipperlabskovs* (Danish goulash; 155kr) are legendary, as is the *smørrebrød* (from 65kr).

KANAL CAFEEN

Frederiksholms Kanal 18 ☎ 33 11 57 70
ⓦ kanalcafeen.dk. Mon–Fri 11.30am–5pm, Sat 11.30am–3pm. MAP P.33, POCKET MAP C13
Founded in 1852, this cosy, historic lunchtime restaurant opposite Christiansborg serves outstanding, good-value smørrebrød (from 53kr for marinated herring). Inside, the decor is all heavy tablecloths and period oil paintings, while outside there's canalside seating in summer.

Bars

OSCAR BAR OG CAFÉ

Rådhuspladsen 77 ☎ 33 12 09 99,
ⓦ oscarbarcafe.dk. Sun–Thurs 11am–11pm, Fri & Sat 11am–2am. MAP P.33, POCKET MAP B13
Set just next to the Rådhus, this very popular gay bar is lively and well-lit, and has DJs pumping tunes out until late on weekends. Happy hour (5–9pm) has 33kr Carlsbergs, and there are good sandwiches and burgers (from 79kr) too.

Venues

MOJO

Løngangstræde 21C ☎ 33 11 64 53, ⓦ mojo .dk. Daily 8pm–5am. MAP P.33, POCKET MAP C13
This authentic, smoky bar with sticky beer-stained tables is a must for blues aficionados. The live gigs (most nights from 9.30pm) are usually free, though chargeable (up to 100kr) when bigger names are playing.

GRØFTEN

Strøget and the Inner City

Indre By ("inner city") is Copenhagen's heart and hub, its compact warren of narrow streets and cobbled squares home to the capital's principal shopping district and countless bars and restaurants. For centuries Indre By was Copenhagen, springing into life with the arrival of Bishop Absolon in 1167, and fortified with stone walls until the nineteenth century. Historic buildings rub shoulders with modern but the area, bisected by the bustling pedestrianized thoroughfare of Strøget, is at its most atmospheric around the Latin Quarter, original home to the university, and pretty, colourful Gråbrødre Torv.

STRØGET

MAP PP.40–41, POCKET MAP B12–D11

The principal artery of the city's main shopping district, **Strøget** is a series of five interconnecting pedestrian streets, over 1km in length, which runs from Rådhuspladsen to Kongens Nytorv (see p.42). One of the world's first pedestrian strips when it was created in 1962, it's abuzz with life 24/7 from the constant flow of shoppers during the day and revellers at night. Street entertainers and fruit and snack sellers also ply their trade – the weeks before Christmas are especially lively, with carol singers, shoppers galore and delicious treats – such as *æbleskiver* (sweet, deep-fried apple dumplings) and *gløgg* (mulled wine) on sale.

The Rådhuspladsen end of Strøget, beginning with **Frederiksberggade**, is fairly tacky but the strip gradually goes more upmarket, running past some of the city's oldest buildings and squares. On **Gammeltorv** (Old Square), look out for the **Caritas Fountain**, which predates the (much more famous) Manneken Pis in Brussels, and features a woman spraying water from her breasts as a small boy pees into the basin.

AMAGERTORV

From here, Strøget continues past Amagertorv (see p.41), culminating in a line of exclusive designer stores as it reaches Østergade and Kongens Nytorv (see p.42).

RUNDETÅRN

Købmagergade 52A ☎ 33 73 03 73, ⓦ rundetaarn.dk. Tower: daily mid-May to Sept 10am–8pm, Oct to mid-May 10am–5pm. Observatory: mid-Oct to mid-March Tues & Wed 7–10pm. 25kr. MAP PP.40–41, POCKET MAP C11

Built by Christian IV in the mid-seventeenth century, the 42m-high **Rundetårn** (Round Tower) originally formed part of a larger complex, functioning both as church tower and **observatory**. The observatory, at the top of the tower, is still operational – the oldest of its kind still in use in Europe – and can be visited in wintertime, while the ascent, along a wide, cobbled walkway, is straightforward even for vertigo sufferers. As you make your way up, you can catch your breath at the **modern art gallery** in the former university library hall, and at the various other quirky exhibits en route, including Christian IV's toilet. The view from the top, across the city's many towers and spires, is fabulous.

RUNDETÅRN

THE LATIN QUARTER

Frue Plads. MAP PP.40–41, POCKET MAP B11

In one of the city's most historic areas, the buildings of the so-called **Latin Quarter** around Fiolstræde date back to the foundation of Scandinavia's earliest university in 1475. Hailing from 1836, the grand neogothic **university** building across Frue Plads from Vor Frue Kirke serves a primarily administrative purpose today – most of the university departments have relocated outside the city centre. On one side a row of busts of the university's rationalist scholars – including Nobel prize-winning Niels Bohr – faces off against busts of religious men lining the cathedral wall opposite.

HELLIGÅNDSKIRKEN

Amagertorv. Mon–Fri noon–4pm (plus services on Sun). MAP PP.40–41, POCKET MAP C12

One of the city's oldest churches, dating back to the thirteenth century, the **Helligåndskirken** (Church of the Holy Ghost) was originally part of a Catholic monastery. Following the Reformation it became a Lutheran church, and although repeatedly destroyed (by fire and bombardment), an evocative section of the monastery, the **Helligånd-shuset**, survives in the church's west wing (to the left of the entrance) as the city's largest and most intact medieval building. It's not hard to imagine its past incarnation as a medieval hospital, beds crammed in between the slender granite columns that hold up the heavy vaulted ceiling. Today it houses regular flea markets and exhibitions.

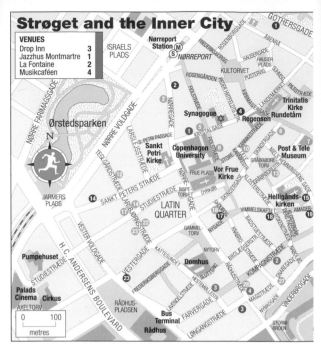

Strøget and the Inner City

VENUES	
Drop Inn	3
Jazzhus Montmartre	1
La Fontaine	2
Musikcaféen	4

VOR FRUE KIRKE

Frue Plads ☎ 33 15 10 78,
🌐 koebenhavnsdomkirke.dk. Daily 8am–5pm,
except during services. MAP ABOVE, POCKET MAP B11

The plain, rather sombre-looking **Vor Frue Kirke** (Church of Our Lady) dates from 1829 and has functioned as Copenhagen's cathedral since 1923, though there's been a church on this site since the eleventh century. It's not until you're through the heavy Doric-pillared portal into the whitewashed Neoclassical interior that its more elegant features are revealed. A simple carved frieze above the altar accentuates a magnificent statue of Christ by Bertel Thorvaldsen (see p.55); the statue's hand positioning gave Thorvaldsen much grief before he finally decided on the open

downward-facing position appreciated by both Catholics and Protestants alike. In 2004, the cathedral briefly hit the international spotlight as the

VOR FRUE KIRKE

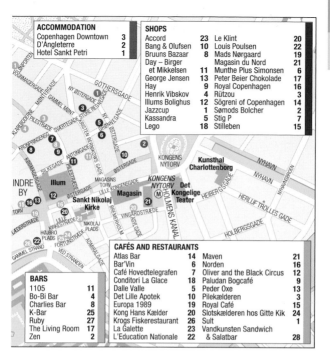

ACCOMMODATION	
Copenhagen Downtown	3
D'Angleterre	2
Hotel Sankt Petri	1

SHOPS	
Accord	23
Bang & Olufsen	10
Bruuns Bazaar	8
Day – Birger et Mikkelsen	11
George Jensen	13
Hay	9
Henrik Vibskov	4
Illums Bolighus	12
Jazzcup	1
Kassandra	5
Lego	18
Le Klint	20
Louis Poulsen	22
Mads Nørgaard	19
Magasin du Nord	21
Munthe Plus Simonsen	6
Peter Beier Chokolade	17
Royal Copenhagen	16
Rützou	3
Søgreni of Copenhagen	14
Sømods Bolcher	2
Stig P	7
Stilleben	15

CAFÉS AND RESTAURANTS	
Atlas Bar	14
Bar'Vin	6
Café Hovedtelegrafen	7
Conditori La Glace	18
Dalle Valle	5
Det Lille Apotek	10
Europa 1989	19
Kong Hans Kælder	20
Krogs Fiskerestaurant	26
La Galette	23
L'Education Nationale	22
Maven	21
Norden	16
Oliver and the Black Circus	12
Paludan Bogcafé	9
Peder Oxe	13
Pilekælderen	3
Royal Café	15
Slotskælderen hos Gitte Kik	24
Sult	1
Vandkunsten Sandwich & Salatbar	28

BARS	
1105	11
Bo-Bi Bar	4
Charlies Bar	8
K-Bar	25
Ruby	27
The Living Room	17
Zen	2

venue for the wedding of Crown Prince Frederik and his Tasmanian wife Mary.

AMAGERTORV AND HØJBRO PLADS

MAP ABOVE, POCKET MAP C12–D12

If Strøget has a focal point, it's the L-shaped interconnecting squares of **Amagertorv** and **Højbro Plads**. On the direct route between the once royal residence of Christiansborg and Vor Frue Kirke these two squares have borne witness to numerous coronation parties, royal weddings and (prior to the Reformation) religious processions. They're especially bustling in summertime when the cafés set up outside and snack vendors and bicycle rickshaw operators ply their trade. Tourists seem perpetually drawn to pose by the two artworks by sculptor Vilhem Bissen: an equestrian statue of Bishop Absalon and the *Storkespringvandet* (Stork Fountain), while a more recent addition is the beautiful mosaic paving by Bjørn Nørgaard (see p.53).

KØBMAGERGADE AND AROUND

MAP ABOVE, POCKET MAP D11

On the corner of Strøget and the busy pedestrianized side street of **Købmagergade**, the Illum department store is one of the city's top places to shop, full of labels including Acne and Paul Smith. Running off Købmagergade to the east is a super-trendy knot of lanes – most notably **Pilestræde** – littered with exclusive designer shops.

STRØGET

POST & TELE MUSEUM

Købmagergade 37 ☎ 33 41 09 00,
🌐 ptt-museum.dk. Daily 10am–4pm. Free.
MAP PP.40–41, POCKET MAP C11

The **Post & Tele Museum** is
devoted to the history of
communication, from the
establishment of the country's
first post office in 1624 (another
Scandinavian first) up to now,
taking in floors and floors of old
stagecoaches, early computers
and probably the best stamp
collection in the world en route.
Most fascinating is the – by its
nature – constantly changing
exhibition on the future of
communications, though best of
all is the wonderful rooftop café
(see p.46) that offers fine views
of downtown Copenhagen.

KONGENS NYTORV

MAP PP.40–41, POCKET MAP E11

The city's grandest square,
Kongens Nytorv was for years
the main entrance to the royal
part of the city. It is currently
largely hidden behind a metro
construction site, and unlikely
to be accessible before 2017.
The "King's New Square" was
laid out in 1670 by Christian V
as part of a large urban
expansion project. A 1688-era
bronze statue of him thus

stands at its centre – the oldest
equestrian statue in Scandinavia, in fact. You'll also come
across a copper-clad Baroque
telephone kiosk from 1913.

DET KONGELIGE TEATER

Kongens Nytorv ☎ 33 69 69 33, 🌐 kglteater
.dk. Tours (in Danish only) roughly every other
Sun 11am; 75kr MAP PP.40–41, POCKET MAP E11

Somewhat confusingly, **Det
Kongelige Teater** (the Royal
Theatre) comprises three
buildings: the main building
on Kongens Nytorv, the Opera
House on Holmen (see p.82)
and the Skuespilhuset (see
p.61). Built in 1874, the
Kongens Nytorv theatre is by
far the oldest of the three, and
for years was the country's
main national performance
venue, hosting opera, ballet
and drama under one roof
– though today it is primarily
used for ballet. As a fourteen-
year-old Hans Christian
Andersen is known to have
tried his luck as a ballet dancer
here though the audition was,
by all accounts, a disaster.
There are occasional guided
tours of the theatre though to
fully experience its grandeur
you'll have to watch a
performance.

Shops

ACCORD

Vestergade 37 ☎ 70 15 16 17, ⓦ accord.dk.
Mon–Thurs 10am–6pm, Fri 10am–7pm, Sat
10am–4pm, Sun noon–5pm. MAP PP.40–41,
POCKET MAP B12

This secondhand music store
buys and sells vinyl records
galore, and is a popular
weekend hangout among
fortysomething nostalgists,
though there's plenty here for
younger folk too.

BANG & OLUFSEN

Østergade 18 ☎ 33 11 14 15,
ⓦ bang-olufsen.com. Mon–Thurs 10am–6pm,
Fri 10am–7pm, Sat 10am–4pm. MAP PP.40–41,
POCKET MAP D11

At B&O's sleek flagship store
you can check out their latest
top-of-the-range sound and
vision kit: good to look at even
if might stretch beyond your
holiday budget. A pair of
super-lightweight headphones
in funky colours will set you
back 845kr.

BRUUNS BAZAAR

Kronprinsensgade 8–9 ☎ 33 77 00 77,
ⓦ bruunsbazaar.dk. Mon–Fri 10am–6pm, Sat
11am–4pm. MAP PP.40–41, POCKET MAP C11

Two minimalist neighbouring
stores selling simple, stylish
and beautifully made clothes
– ladies' at no. 8, gents' at
no. 9 – created by in-house
designers, hence the somewhat
hefty price tag.

DAY – BIRGER ET MIKKELSEN

Pilestræde 16 ☎ 33 45 88 80, ⓦ day.dk.
Mon–Fri 10am–6pm, Sat 11am–4pm.
MAP PP.40–41, POCKET MAP D11

A two-storey fashion house
selling own-design women's
garb with a colourful, ethnic
twist. Prices from 700kr
for a stripy t-shirt up to the
4500kr mark for a glittery
cocktail dress.

GEORGE JENSEN

Amagertorv 4 ☎ 33 11 40 80, ⓦ georgejensen
.dk. Mon–Thurs 10am–6pm, Fri 10am–7pm,
Sat 10am–5pm. MAP PP.40–41, POCKET MAP D12

Silverware designed in the
spirit and style of the
celebrated silversmith Georg
Jensen, who first became
known for his Art Nouveau-
style jewellery in the early
twentieth century. A small
museum inside tells his story.

HAY

Pilestræde 29–31 ☎ 42 82 08 20,
ⓦ hayshop.dk. Mon–Fri 10am–6pm, Sat
10am–5pm. MAP PP.40–41, POCKET MAP D11

Colourful, funky household
accessories, including furniture
and rugs, mostly by cutting-
edge Danish designers. A
stunning modular sofa in grey
wool will cost you 16,000kr.

HENRIK VIBSKOV

Krystalgade 6 ☎ 33 14 61 00,
ⓦ henrikvibskovboutique.com. Mon–Thurs
11am–6pm, Fri 11am–7pm, Sat 11am–5pm.
MAP PP.40–41, POCKET MAP C11

Weird and wonderful (and
pricey) gear from Copenhagen's *enfant terrible* clothes
designer. Henrik, also an artist
and drummer, is notorious for
his colourful, flamboyant and
über-trendy men's and
women's wear.

SHOPPING ON STRØGET

ILLUMS BOLIGHUS

Amagertorv 10 ☎ 33 14 19 41,
🌐 illumsbolighus.dk. Mon–Fri 10am–7pm, Sat
10am–6pm, Sun 11am–5pm. MAP PP.40–41,
POCKET MAP D12

A Copenhagen institution, this gorgeous design department store sells everything from top-of-the-range clothes to furniture and kitchenware from global designer icons. It's also the place to go year-round for beautiful Christmas decorations.

JAZZCUP

Gothersgade 107 ☎ 33 33 87 40,
🌐 jazzklubben.dk. Tues–Thurs 10am–5.30pm,
Fri 10am–6pm, Sat 10am–2pm, Sun
11am–5pm. MAP PP.40–41, POCKET MAP C10

Excellent music store specializing in jazz, blues, soul and world music. It also has a small café and hosts the occasional live gig.

KASSANDRA

Grønnegade 27 ☎ 33 91 08 89, Mon–Thurs
11am–6pm, Fri 11am–7pm, Sat 10am–4pm.
MAP PP.40–41, POCKET MAP D11

One of the city's most beloved shoe stores, with scores of the latest heels from highbrow labels that include Jimmy Choo, Stella McCartney, Chloé and Pedro Garcia. Also sells bags from the same designers.

LEGO

Vimmelskaftet 37 🌐 stores.lego.com.
Mon–Thurs & Sat 10am–6pm, Fri 10am–7pm.
MAP PP.40–41, POCKET MAP C12

A must for Lego connoisseurs of all ages, the flagship store even provides building tips and tricks, and can get you replacement pieces for those crucial ones you've lost from the colourful and never-ending Pick-a-Brick wall.

LE KLINT

Store Kirkestræde 1 ☎ 33 11 66 63,

HENRIK VIBSKOV

🌐 leklint.com. Tues–Fri 10am–6pm, Sat
10am–4pm. MAP PP.40–41, POCKET MAP D12

Originally started by famous furniture designer Kaare Klint, Le Klint's lamps are now a globally sought-after brand. The current in-house designers have maintained his simple, aesthetic style.

LOUIS POULSEN

Gammel Strand 28 ☎ 70 33 14 14,
🌐 louispoulsen.com. Mon–Thurs 8am–4pm,
Fri 8am–3.30pm. MAP PP.40–41, POCKET MAP D12

Beautiful lighting from top designers past and present including Poul Henningsen whose famous glare-free PH lamps, made up of concentric circular metal shades, were launched in this store many moons ago.

MADS NØRGAARD

Amagertorv 13–15 ☎ 33 32 01 28,
🌐 madsnorgaard.com. Mon–Thurs 10am–6pm,
Fri 10am–7pm, Sat 11am–4pm. MAP PP.40–41,
POCKET MAP C12

Good-quality, own-design everyday wear for women and children (at no. 13) and men (no. 15) in cheerful, often stripy colours. Prices are reasonable for what you get.

MAGASIN DU NORD

Kongens Nytorv 13 ☎ 33 11 44 33,
ⓦ magasin.dk. Daily 10am–8pm. MAP PP.40–41,
POCKET MAP E12

This age-old department store is still going strong, selling top-notch clothes and homeware. Head to the basement for the gourmet food hall, well stocked with organic and fair-trade foodstuffs and wines, You'll also find magazines and newspapers from around the globe down here.

MUNTHE PLUS SIMONSEN

Grønnegade 10 ☎ 33 32 00 12,
ⓦ muntheplusmandshsnen.dk. Mon–Thurs 10am–4pm, Fri 10am–7pm, Sat 10am–4pm. MAP PP.40–41, POCKET MAP D11

Pricey and exciting – bordering on grungy – women's clothing, designed by Naja Munthe. Known for its exquisite details, feminine lines and high-quality materials the collection is completely renewed every three months.

PETER BEIER CHOKOLADE

Skoubogade 1 ☎ 33 93 07 17,
ⓦ peterbeierchokolade.dk. Mon–Thurs 10am–6pm, Fri 10am–7pm, Sat 10am–4pm. MAP PP.40–41, POCKET MAP B12

Wonderful selection of handmade chocolates, put together with the finest ingredients. The cocoa comes from their own plantation in the Caribbean.

ROYAL COPENHAGEN

Amagertorv 6 ☎ 3313 7181,
ⓦ royalcopenhagen.com. Mon–Fri 10am–7pm, Sat 10am–5pm, Sun 11am–5pm. MAP PP.40–41, POCKET MAP C12

Flagship store for the Royal Porcelain Factory's famous china, distinguished by its blue patterning. The beautiful gabled store building, from 1616, is one of the city's oldest, having survived countless city-centre fires. Prices start at 299kr for a decorated egg cup.

RÜTZOU

Store Regnegade 3 ☎ 70 23 06 16,
ⓦ rutzou.com. Mon–Thurs 11am–5.30pm, Fri 11am–6pm, Sat 10am–4pm. MAP PP.40–41, POCKET MAP D11

Floaty bordering on ethnic designer wear for women by Susanne Rützou, who finds her inspiration in contemporary art. The simple and uncluttered store in wood, glass and concrete provides the perfect setting for her beautiful clothes.

SÖGRENI OF COPENHAGEN

Sankt Peders Stræde 30A ☎ 33 12 78 79,
ⓦ sogrenibikes.com. Mon–Fri 10am–6pm, Sat 10am–4pm. MAP PP.40–41, POCKET MAP A12

Sögreni's beautiful handmade bikes are assembled in store, though with prices starting at around 12,000kr they don't come cheap. It's a great place for bike accessories, such as chain guards and lights, which are also designed and crafted in-house. Items begin at around 290kr for a pretty little copper bell.

PETER BEIER CHOKOLADE

SØMODS BOLCHER

Nørregade 36 ☎ 33 12 60 46, ⓦ soemods
-bolcher.dk. Mon–Thurs 9.15am–5.30pm, Fri
9.15am–6pm, Sat 10am–2.30pm, Sun
11am–3pm. MAP PP.40–41, POCKET MAP B11

Dinky little confectioner that
uses age-old methods – dating
back to its establishment in
1891 – to produce beautiful
boiled and hand-rolled candy
in myriad colours and flavours.

STIG P

Kronprinsensgade 14 ☎ 33 14 42 16
ⓦ stigpdk. Mon–Thurs 10.30am–6pm, Fri
10.30am–7pm, Sat 10am–5pm. MAP PP.40–41,
POCKET MAP D11

This colourful, welcoming
women's clothes store was the
first to open on trendy
Kronprinsensgade, way back in
1969. Designer wear encompasses Stella McCartney, Calvin
Klein and Stig P's own label.

STILLEBEN

Niels Hemmingsensgade 3 ☎ 33 91 11 31.
ⓦ stillebenshop.com. Mon–Fri 10am–6pm,
Sat 10am–4pm. MAP PP.40–41, POCKET MAP C12

Funky ceramics, glass, textiles
and much, much more from
mostly Danish designers. They
seem to specialize in quirky
items that, once seen, you'll
never be able live without.

STILLEBEN

Cafés and restaurants

ATLAS BAR

Larsbjørnsstræde 18 ☎ 33 15 03 52,
ⓦ atlasbar.dk. Mon–Sat noon–10pm.
MAP PP.40–41, POCKET MAP B12

Informal café-cum-restaurant
serving affordable dishes from
around the globe in a
charming, laid-back setting.
There's an extensive vegetarian
menu (including delicious nut
burgers made with hazelnuts,
carrots and celeriac;
100kr/125kr for lunch/dinner)
with a good range of freshly
made salads, and lots of freshly
squeezed juices, too.

BAR'VIN

Skindergade 3 ☎ 34 05 87 33, ⓦ barvin.dk.
Mon–Thurs 11.30am–11pm, Fri–Sat
11.30am–midnight. MAP PP.40–41, POCKET MAP C11

The menu at this rustic, relaxed
wine bar changes to match the
wine (rather than the other way
around), though the delicious
charcuterie and cheese platters
are always a good bet. From
85kr for a sandwich up to
285kr for a three-course meal.

CAFÉ HOVEDTELEGRAFEN

Købmagergade 37 ☎ 33 41 09 86,
ⓦ cafehovedtelegrafen.dk. Daily 10am–4pm.
MAP PP.40–41, POCKET MAP C11

With great views across the city
spires, this bright and airy
café-restaurant on the top floor
of the Post & Tele Museum
serves smørrebrød to die for
(from 89kr), plus excellent
salads and well-made
sandwiches. When the weather
permits, there's also seating out
on the balcony.

CONDITORI LA GLACE

Skoubogade 3 ☎ 33 14 46 46, ⓦ laglace.dk.
Mon–Thurs 8.30am–5.30pm, Fri 8.30am–6pm,

EUROPA 1989

Sat 9am–5pm, Sun 10am–5pm (closed Sun April–Sept). MAP PP.40–41, POCKET MAP B12

Traditional patisserie serving beautifully crafted layer cakes and pastries. Try the scrumptious HC Hat cake, made with chocolate, caramel mousse and lemon ganache (52kr per slice).

DALLE VALLE

Fiolstræde 3–5 ☎ 33 93 29 29, Ⓦ cafedallevalle.dk. Mon–Thurs 10am–midnight, Fri & Sat 10am–3am, Sun 10am–11pm. MAP PP.40–41, POCKET MAP B11

This spacious and always bustling café is a great place for sandwiches and salads, with a few pasta dishes, burgers and steaks also on offer; scrummy hot wings, too (15kr). Also a popular bar at night, with a DJ on Friday and Saturday.

DET LILLE APOTEK

Store Kannikestræde 15 ☎ 33 12 56 06, Ⓦ detlilleapotek.dk. Daily 11.30am–midnight. MAP PP.40–41, POCKET MAP C11

Dating back to 1720, the city's oldest restaurant was once one of H.C. Andersen's favourite haunts, and with its leadlight windows and hanging oil lamps it still retains plenty of old-time atmosphere. Highlights on the menu of traditional Danish dishes include *biksemad* (beef stew served with pickled beetroot, cucumber salad, fried eggs and slices of rye bread;

98kr) for lunch and *flæskesteg* (pork roast with crackling, sugar-glazed potatoes, pickled red cabbage and a thick, creamy sauce; 159kr) for dinner.

EUROPA 1989

Amagertorv 1 ☎ 33 14 28 89, Ⓦ europa1989.dk. Mon–Thurs 7.45am–11pm, Fri & Sat 7.45am–1am, Sun 9am–10pm. MAP PP.40–41, POCKET MAP D12

Large, fancy café on bustling Højbro Plads serving excellent coffee and cake. It's also a good stop for breakfast (wholegrain porridge 39kr) and brunch (daily until 3pm; 119kr), and a popular meet-after-work spot, though mostly for the drinks (a good selection of beer) and their excellent European nibbles; try the shellfish bisque or *bruschetta*.

KONG HANS KÆLDER

Vingårdstræde 6 ☎ 33 11 68 68, Ⓦ konghans.dk. Mon–Sat 6pm–midnight. MAP PP.40–41, POCKET MAP D12

Set in the cellar of a medieval merchant's house, this Michelin-starred place has a setting as dramatic as it is romantic. The picture-perfect food is French-inspired with a twist. The eight-course menu will set you back a mere 1150kr, not including wine, while an à la carte main starts at 475kr.

KROGS FISKERESTAURANT

Gammel Strand 38 ☎ 33 15 89 15, ⓦ krogs
.dk. Mon–Sat noon–3pm & 6pm–midnight.
MAP PP.40–41, POCKET MAP C12

Though hidden behind the
metro building chaos, the
grande dame of the city's
seafood restaurants – all high
stuccoed ceilings and
meticulously dressed tables – is
worth the hassle to get to. Half
a dozen French oysters will set
you back 195kr, or – if you're
feeling flush – try the lobster
with all the trimmings (425kr).

LA GALETTE

Larsbjørnsstræde 9 ☎ 33 32 37 90,
ⓦ lagalette.dk. Mon–Sat noon–4pm &
5.30–10pm, Sun 4–10pm. MAP PP.40–41,
POCKET MAP B12

Informal place serving
French-style buckwheat
pancakes with both sweet and
savoury fillings. Specialities
include the Menez-Hom (85kr),
filled with goat's cheese, walnuts
and salad, and the Normande
(60kr) with calvados-flambéed
caramelized apples. In summer
there's outdoor seating in the
back yard.

L'EDUCATION NATIONALE

Larsbjørnsstræde 12 ☎ 33 91 53 60,
ⓦ leducation.dk. Mon–Sat 11.30am–midnight,
Sun 4.30–10pm. MAP PP.40–41, POCKET MAP B12

Authentic and cosy, French-
style bistro with tightly packed
tables and French-speaking
waiters. Lunchtime standards,
such as omelette (85kr) and
moules marinières (89kr), are
very reasonably priced. The
evening menu is pricier but still
good value (mains such as
pheasant or sea bass around
200kr), and there's an excellent
selection of wines.

MAVEN

Nikolaj Plads 10 ☎ 32 20 11 00,
ⓦ restaurantmaven.dk. Mon–Thurs
11.30am–midnight, Fri & Sat 11.30am–2am.
MAP PP.40–41, POCKET MAP D12

Inside the massive, red-brick
Skt Nikolaj Kirke, a deconse-
crated church that also hosts
temporary exhibitions, *Maven*
("stomach") offers excellent
French/Italian-inspired lunch
and dinner menus as well as
traditional lunchtime
smørrebrød (179kr for a
platter). Also a popular spot for
evening drinks.

NORDEN

Østergade 61 ☎ 33 11 77 91, ⓦ cafenorden
.dk. Daily 9am–midnight. MAP PP.40–41,
POCKET MAP D12

A great pit stop on busy Strøget
with fabulous home-made
cakes and pancakes as well as
beautifully assembled salads
(from 145kr). There's also a fine
selection of beer (including
from the Jacobsen brewery; see
p.89), a range of cocktails and a
good few wines.

OLIVER AND THE BLACK CIRCUS

Teglgårdsstræde 8A ☎ 74 56 88 88,
ⓦ oliverandtheblackcircus.com. Tues–Sat
11.30am–2.30pm & 5.30pm–1am. MAP PP.40–41,
POCKET MAP B11

Dark and moody yet cosy, this
eccentric and bohemian new
restaurant decor (check out the
goblins) offers fabulous
starter-sized dishes – such as
cured mackerel and blueberries
or cod roe and bacon – which
you can mix and match to
create your own menu (three/
four/five courses
295/375/440kr).

PALUDAN BOGCAFÉ

Fiolstræde 10–12 ☎ 33 15 06 75,
ⓦ paludan-cafe.dk. Mon–Fri 9am–10pm, Sat
10am–10pm, Sun 10am–8pm. MAP PP.40–41,
POCKET MAP B11

With its free wi-fi and
great-value meals – chicken
tagliatelle (89kr) or the
Paludan burger, for example

– this bookshop-cum-café is a great student hangout. There's also good coffee and cheap beer.

PEDER OXE

Gråbrødretorv 11 ☎ 33 11 00 77, ⓦ pederoxe .dk. Mon–Wed & Sun 11.30am–10.30pm Thurs–Sat 11.30am–11pm. MAP PP.40–41, POCKET MAP C11

One of several cafés and restaurants on this historic square (once home to a Greyfriars monastery), serving juicy, grilled organic burgers (from 135kr) and steaks (195kr) plus unlimited salads (115kr). The "dessert tapas" platter (139kr) is an exquisite experience in itself. Also a good place to go for drinks.

PILEKÆLDEREN

Pilestræde 48 ☎ 33 33 00 26, ⓦ pilekaelderen.dk. Mon–Sat 11.30am–5pm. MAP PP.40–41, POCKET MAP D11

Authentic, traditional lunchtime restaurant with thick stone walls and a low wood-beamed ceiling. It specializes in stunning smørrebrød, such as herring marinated in elderberry

aquavit (64kr) – all home-made, of course.

ROYAL CAFÉ

Amagertorv 6 ☎ 33 12 11 22, ⓦ theroyalcafe .dk. Mon–Fri 10am–7pm, Sat 10am–6pm, Sun 11am–5pm. MAP PP.40–41, POCKET MAP C12

In the courtyard of the Royal Copenhagen flagship store, the *Royal Café* is the originator of "smushi" (sushi smørrebrød), the selection changing with the seasons. Try a platter of three (135kr) or individual pieces for 48kr. Most locals consider these to be the best modern takes on smørrebrød in town. It can get very crowded, especially on weekends, so you might ask for your smushi to go.

SLOTSKÆLDEREN HOS GITTE KIK

Fortunstræde 4 ☎ 33 11 15 37, ⓦ slotskaelderen.dk. Tues–Sat 10am–5pm. MAP PP.40–41, POCKET MAP D12

Cosy basement restaurant serving excellent traditional smørrebrød. Make your choice from the vast selection at the counter, such as delicious *rullepølse* (rolled pork with parsley and pepper), and the food will be brought to your table.

ROYAL CAFÉ

SULT

Vognmagergade 8B ☎ 33 74 34 17,
ⓦ restaurantsult.dk. Tues–Fri noon–10pm, Sat
& Sun 10am–10pm. MAP PP.40–41, POCKET MAP C10

Occupying a high-ceilinged
dining hall in the same building
as the Danish Film Institute,
Sult does simple well-prepared
Danish dishes that don't cost the
earth. Try the mouthwatering
freshly cured ham from Jutland,
served with grilled tomatoes
and artichokes (129kr).

VANDKUNSTEN SANDWICH & SALATBAR

Rådhusstræde 17 ☎ 33 13 90 40,
ⓦ vsandwich.dk. Mon–Sat 10am–4pm.
MAP PP.40–41, POCKET MAP C12

Excellent place to grab a
sandwich on the go (39–49kr),
with lots of yummy vegetarian
options (avocado mousse,
mozzarella and so on) and
freshly baked, crisp Italian
rolls. Salads, which you can
make up yourself, start at 44kr.

Bars

1105

Kristen Bernikows Gade 4 ☎ 33 93 11 05,
ⓦ 1105.dk. Wed, Thurs & Sat 8pm–2am, Fri
4pm–2am. MAP PP.40–41, POCKET MAP D11

Cool, elegant, low-lit cocktail
bar, where the mixologists wear
crisp white lab coats. *1105* has
made a name for itself with the
creation of the Copenhagen
cocktail, a delicious mix of
genever (Dutch gin), cherry
liqueur, lime juice and a host of
secret ingredients.

BO-BI BAR

Klareboderne 4 ☎ 33 12 55 43. Daily
noon–2am. MAP PP.40–41, POCKET MAP C11

This baroque, red hole-in-the-
wall is one of the city's most
authentic watering holes.
Opened in 1917, it sports
Copenhagen's oldest bar
counter and attracts a
refreshingly boho clientele of
writers, students and
intellectuals – great for people
watching. Serves cheap bottles
of great Danish and Czech
beers as well as local schnapps.

CHARLIES BAR

Pilestræde 33 ☎ 33 32 22 89. Mon 2pm–
midnight, Tues & Wed noon–1am,
Thurs–Sat noon–2am, Sun 2–11pm.
MAP PP.40–41, POCKET MAP D11

Packed, small and smoky,
Copenhagen's only UK-style
pub – even boasting Casque
Mark accreditation – draws in
the crowds night after night for
its ever-changing range of
British ales and ciders.

K-BAR

Ved Stranden 20 ☎ 33 91 92 22, ⓦ k-bar.dk.
Mon–Sat 4pm–2am. MAP PP.40–41, POCKET MAP D12

Tucked away around the corner from Højbro Plads, this funky cocktail bar has deep, cosy sofas into which punters can happily sink as they sip the beautiful concoctions of owner Kirsten– hence the K. Try the unusual and very moreish Rissitini, made with gin, sake, lychee liqueur and ginger.

RUBY

Nybrogade 10 ☎ 33 93 12 03, ⓦ rby.dk.
Mon–Sat 4pm–2am, Sun 6pm–midnight.
MAP PP.40–41, POCKET MAP C12

Set in what appears to be for all the world an unassuming ground-floor apartment, with comfy leather armchairs and no obvious signage, this is possibly the city's best cocktail bar. Try the signature Rapscallion – a Scottish take on the Manhattan, with Talisker over a sweet PX sherry.

THE LIVING ROOM

Larsbjørnsstræde 17 ☎ 33 32 66 10.
Mon–Thurs 10am–11pm, Fri 10am–2am, Sat 11am–2am, Sun noon–7pm. MAP PP.40–41,
POCKET MAP B12

Laid-back corner bar on chilled Larsbjørnsstræde, with tables outside and soft sofas in the basement. It's a great place to go for freshly squeezed juices, organic wines, coffee and affordable cocktails.

ZEN

Nørregade 41 ☎ 33 11 00 46, ⓦ zen.dk.
Thurs–Sat 11pm–4am. MAP PP.40–41,
POCKET MAP B11

This chic, exclusive nightclub is run by Denmark's answer to Simon Cowell, meaning one thing: fat beats, pretty young things grinding on the dance floor and oodles of pretension. Go, if you must.

Venues

DROP INN

Kompagnistræde 34 ☎ 33 11 24 04,
ⓦ drop-inn.dk. Mon–Sat noon–5am, Sun 2pm–2am. Usually free Mon–Thurs; Fri & Sat from 30kr MAP PP.40–41, POCKET MAP B12

Small folk, blues and rock venue, with tables spilling onto the pavement during hot summer months and a good selection of international beers. Music from 10/10.30pm most nights (usually free during the week; from 30kr Sat & Sun).

JAZZHUS MONTMARTRE

Store Regnegade 19A ☎ 70 26 32 67,
ⓦ jazzhusmontmartre.dk. Doors open at 5.30pm. MAP PP.40–41, POCKET MAP D11

Intimate, not-for-profit jazz club, recently reopened on its original premises, which placed Copenhagen firmly on the international jazz map in the 1950s when it hosted legends such as Dexter Gordon and Stan Getz. Concerts two to three nights a week (80–350kr).

LA FONTAINE

Kompagnistræde 11 ☎ 33 11 60 98,
ⓦ lafontaine.dk. Daily 8pm–5am.
MAP PP.40–41, POCKET MAP C12

As Copenhagen's oldest jazz venue, *La Fontaine* has for decades been where jazz musicians make for on their nights off. It's small and packed, with live gigs at the weekend (Fri, Sat & Sun from 10.30pm; entry from 60kr).

MUSIKCAFÉEN

Rådhusstræde 13 ☎ 33 69 32 14,
ⓦ huset-kbh.dk. MAP PP.40–41, POCKET MAP C12

On the third floor of the Huset cultural centre, this is the place to hear up-and-coming bands before they become famous. Gigs most nights, starting at 9pm (30–150kr).

Slotsholmen

Encircled by Indre By on three sides and abutting the Inner Harbour on the fourth, the flat, diminutive island of Slotsholmen has been the country's seat of power for almost a thousand years. It was here, in 1167, that Bishop Absalon founded a castle to protect the village's herring traders from Wendish pirates. The area is anchored by the commanding and glum-looking Christiansborg Slot; home to the Danish parliament and the royals' reception rooms, it's the fifth incarnation of a royal dwelling on this site. Other highlights within the palace complex include the extravagant Royal Riding Ground, the elegant Palace Chapel and, next door, the colourful Thorvaldsens Museum, while on the opposite side of Christiansborg the Daniel Libeskind-designed interior of the Danish Jewish Museum and, on the waterfront, the gleaming Black Diamond extension to the Royal Library provide more modern architectural draws.

FOLKETING (DANISH PARLIAMENT)

Christiansborg ☎ 33 37 55 00
ⓦ thedanishparliament.dk. Tours (free) most Sundays at 1pm (tickets available from 10am). Sittings roughly Oct to mid-June: Tues & Wed from 1pm, Thurs & Fri from 10am. MAP P.53, POCKET MAP D13

Occupying the southern half of the three-winged palace of Christiansborg, the **Folketing** (Danish parliament) is a must for fans of the cult TV political drama series *Borgen*, set in and around the palace. You can watch the debates in the principal parliamentary chamber, the **Folketingssal**, when in session – ring the visitors' entrance bell, and, if spaces are available, you'll be taken through security checks to the public galleries – though bear in mind that debates are not nearly as animated as the UK equivalent. Alternatively the Sunday English-language **tours** cover the history of Danish democracy as well as the palace's colourful history, taking you down the long Vandrehal where the much revered original Danish constitution from 1849 is displayed in a silver chest.

ROYAL RECEPTION ROOMS

Christiansborg ☎ 33 92 64 92
ⓦ christiansborg.dk. May–Sept daily 10am–5pm, Oct–April Thurs–Sun 10am–5pm; closed during royal functions. 80kr, 110kr for combined ticket with Ruins under Christiansborg and Royal Stables. Tours at 3pm. MAP P.53, POCKET MAP D12

Although it was built as a royal palace, the royals have never actually lived at Christiansborg, favouring the slightly more open and accessible Amalienborg. A section of the northern wing of the palace is however still in royal use for official functions as the **Royal Reception Rooms** (Det Kongelige Repræsentationslokaler) accessed via the Inner Courtyard. Sure to impress any visiting dignitaries, all the rooms

ROYAL RECEPTION ROOMS

are beautifully adorned. An intricate marble frieze depicting Alexander's march into Babylon by Thorvaldsen (see p.55) was recovered from the previous Christiansborg and following skilful restoration is on display in the Alexander Hall. The marble walls in the oval Throne Room are clad in delicate silks from Lyon, while on the ceiling a magnificent painting depicts

the origins of the national flag. Best of all, however, is the long Great Hall, lined with seventeen magnificent tapestries by Bjørn Nørgaard (also famous for the mosaics on Strøget; see p.41). A fiftieth birthday present for the current Queen, they depict the country's history from the Viking Age to the present. See if you can spot The Beatles and Mao Zedong.

RUINERNE UNDER CHRISTIANSBORG (CASTLE RUINS)

Christiansborg ☎ 33 92 64 92,
ⓦ christiansborg.dk. Ruins closed for
renovation at time of writing (due to open
Jan, 2014). For latest hours check website.
MAP P.53, POCKET MAP D12

The **ruins** of Slotsholmen's two earliest castles have been excavated and now form part of an underground **exhibition** beneath Christiansborg, accessed via a stairwell from the main entrance portal. A walkway tracks the foundations of Bishop Absalon's original castle, while the extant highlight of its successor, Københavns Slot, which was put up in the late fourteenth century, is the foundations of its notorious Blue Tower prison where King Christian IV's daughter Leonora Christine was kept captive for 22 years, supposedly due to her blinding beauty.

RIDEBANE (ROYAL STABLES)

Christiansborg Ridebane 12 ☎ 33 92 64 92,
ⓦ christiansborg.dk. May–Sept daily
1.30–4pm Oct–April Tues–Sun 1.30–4pm;
40kr, 110kr for combined ticket with Royal
Reception Rooms and Ruins under
Christiansborg. Tours in Danish Sat at 2pm.
MAP P.53, POCKET MAP C13

Beyond the Inner Courtyard, the **Ridebane** (Royal Riding Ground) and surrounding Riding Hall and stables are all that's left of the opulent Baroque palace that stood here from 1738 until it burnt to the ground 56 years later. If you arrive around mid-morning you stand a good chance of seeing the Queen's horses being exercised either in the outdoor riding arena, or, if you poke your head in discreetly, in the lavish Riding Hall.

The **Museet Kongelige Stalde og Kareter** (Museum of Royal Stables and Coaches), in the southern flank, houses the extravagant marble-clad stables where a few lucky horses are still kept, alongside the royal collection of gilded carriages plus the previous king's beautiful old Bentley.

To the west as you exit the museum, the Baroque **Marmorbroen** (Marble Bridge) linking Slotsholmen with mainland Indre By was the original palace's main approach.

CHRISTIANSBORG SLOTSKIRKE (PALACE CHAPEL)

Prins Jørgens Gård 1 ⓦ christiansborg.dk.
July daily 10am–5pm, Aug–June Sun
10am–5pm. Tours in Danish Sun at 2pm.
MAP P.53, POCKET MAP D12

Fully restored following a catastrophic fire in 1992 the Neoclassical **Palace Chapel** is all that remains of the second Christiansborg palace, which like its predecessor also burnt to the ground some fifty-odd years after completion (in 1833). The palace was said to be the most lavish of all the Christiansborg incarnations, though the church's elegant and light interior – topped by a vast white dome with four angels in

ROYAL STABLES

Royalty Danish style

The Danish Royal Family stands as one of the oldest monarchies in the world. The current monarch, Her Majesty Queen Margrethe II, traces her lineage all the way back to Harald Bluetooth, the famous Viking chieftain and first king of a united Denmark over a thousand years ago. The Royal Family remains an extremely popular institution across the country. Crown Prince Frederik has been regularly voted "Dane of The Year", while his Tasmanian-born wife Princess Mary, who recently gave birth to twins, is a vaunted style icon. In January 2012, Queen Margrethe celebrated 40 years on the throne, during which the Royal Couple went on a pomp-and-circumstance carriage tour from their home, the Amalienborg Palace, all throughout Copenhagen.

relief seemingly floating beneath – is exquisite Classical simplicity itself. Still put to use for the opening of parliament service and for the occasional royal event, such as the baptism of the Crown Prince's first child in 2006, the church is also used for organ practice by the Danish Music Conservatory.

THORVALDSENS MUSEUM

Bertel Thorvaldsens Plads 2 ☎ 33 32 15 32, ⓦ thorvaldsensmuseum.dk. Tues–Sun 10am–5pm. 40kr. MAP P.53, POCKET MAP C12

Dedicated to Denmark's most internationally celebrated sculptor, the **Thorvaldsens Museum** is an absorbing place to while away a few hours. You certainly won't miss the grand Neoclassical edifice, overlooking the picturesque Frederiksholms Kanal, within which it's housed: with its striking ochre facade, and unusual slanting doors and window frames, it stands out as one of the city's most original buildings.

Having trained in Copenhagen, **Bertel Thorvaldsen** (1770–1844) spent forty years fulfilling high-profile commissions in Rome before returning triumphantly in 1839 – an event depicted on the huge frieze painted on the canal-facing side of the building. Thorvaldsen spent the last few years of his life fulfilling commissions in Copenhagen, and his work can be seen in both Vor Frue Kirke and Christiansborg Slotskirke.

Inside, richly decorated walls and mosaic floors provide a fitting backdrop for the vast collection of Thorvaldsen's works on the ground floor, from huge marble sculptures to sketches and grubby plaster casts with the sculptor's own original marks. Highlights include the intimate *Cupid and Psyche* and Thorvaldsen's own self-portrait in stone. Upstairs, the sculptor's fine collection of Greek, Roman and Egyptian antiquities is on display.

TØJHUSMUSEET

Tøjhusgade 2 ☏ 33 11 60 37, ⊛ thm.dk.
Daily 11am–5pm. 60kr, Wed free. MAP P.53,
POCKET MAP D13

Whether you're a fan of
weapons or not, the **Tøjhusmuseet** (Royal Danish Arsenal
Museum), occupying the
arsenal of the old Copenhagen
Castle (a forerunner of
Christiansborg), is a treasure-
trove for arms buffs. There are
rows and rows of swords and
firearms on display. Most
remarkable, though, is the
156m arched hall housing the
cannon collection, said to be
the longest such hall in Europe.

BØRSEN

Børsgade. MAP P.53, POCKET MAP D13

A fanciful riot of gables,
pinnacles and grey-green
copper, the red-brick **Børsen**
building is one of the more
remarkable monuments of
Christian IV's reign. It's for its
wonderfully whimsical spire –
made up of the intertwined tails
of four sculpted dragons – that
the building is best known. The
dragons supposedly protect the
Børsen from attack and fire,
and seem to be fulfilling their
duties quite successfully as the
building has survived many a
skirmish as those around it
have burnt to the ground.
Although ownership of the
building has long since passed
to the Chamber of Commerce
(it's not open to the public), the
dragon spire remains the official
symbol of the Danish stock
exchange.

DANSK JØDISK MUSEUM

Proviantpassagen 6 ☏ 33 11 22 18,
⊛ jewmus.dk. June-Aug Tues–Sun
10am–5pm, Sept–May Tues–Fri 1–4pm, Sat &
Sun noon–5pm. 50kr. MAP P.53, POCKET MAP D13

Opened in 2004 and designed
by Daniel Libeskind, architect
of the new World Trade Center
site in New York, the **Danish
Jewish Museum** retells the
story of Jewry in Denmark
from their arrival in the
seventeenth century at the
invitation of Christian IV up to
the gruesome wartime period.
Housed in the Galajhus (Royal
Boat House), the building gives
no indication from the outside
of its subtly disorientating
interior, a labyrinth of fractured
passageways and sloping floors
reminiscent of Libeskind's
more famous Jewish Museum
in Berlin. The museum's layout
corresponds to the interlocking
characters of the Hebrew word
Mitzvah ("good deed"), a
reference to the Danes'
smuggling of seven thousand
Jews hidden away in fishing
boats across to sanctuary in
Sweden during World War II
(see box, p.62).

The exhibition itself is divided
into five sections, focusing on
different aspects of Danish-
Jewish life. The most captivating
of these is the Mitzvah section
itself, which recounts the plight
of Danish Jews during Nazi
occupation. There are some

DANSK JØDISK MUSEUM

heartfelt and touching letters and photos from refugees in Sweden on show, and hand-drawn sketches of horrible episodes at the Theresienstadt concentration camp (in what's now the Czech Republic), where 481 Danish Jews were sent.

DEN SORTE DIAMANT (THE BLACK DIAMOND)

Søren Kierkegaards Plads 1 ☎ 33 47 48 80, Ⓦ kb.dk. Mon–Sat 8am–9pm. Access to all museums 40kr. Tours Sat 3pm 40kr (including access to all museums). MAP P.53, POCKET MAP D13

Den Sorte Diamant (The Black Diamond), a monumental slab of black Zimbabwean granite and glass that leans over (and glitters magically in) the waters of the Inner Harbour below, is one of the city's great modern architectural icons. Completed in 1999, the building is an extension to the Italian-inspired **Kongelige Bibliotek** (Royal Library) (1906), to which it is connected by a futuristic glass-enclosed bridge.

The building houses an auditorium with outstanding acoustics, museums dedicated to photography and cartoon art, and a changing display of works from the Royal Library's collection. You're free to wander around at will (though some exhibitions require an entrance fee).

The old library building behind is less accessible to the general public and best experienced on the **guided tours**, which take in both buildings. Highlights of the Royal Library include several of the atmospheric old study halls, one featuring the city's earliest grid-powered electric lamps.

Shop

DIAMANTINFORMATIONEN

Søren Kierkegaards Plads 1 ☎ 33 47 48 80, Ⓦ kb.dk. Mon–Sat 8am–9pm. MAP P.53, POCKET MAP D13

Selling books, posters and merchandise primarily relating to the Black Diamond's current exhibitions, this is also a good place to shop for books on the city's contemporary architecture.

Café and restaurant

CAFÉ ØIEBLIKKET

Søren Kierkegaards Plads 1 ☎ 33 47 41 06 Ⓦ oieblikket.dk. Mon–Fri 8am–7pm, Sat 9am–6pm. MAP P.53, POCKET MAP D13

A popular venue among the city's studious, the café in the Black Diamond's light and airy foyer offers excellent coffee and an array of mouthwatering cakes. There are deckchairs on the Inner Harbour quayside in summer, too.

SØREN K

Kierkegaards Plads 1 ☎ 33 47 49 49 Ⓦ soerenk.dk. Mon–Sat noon–4pm & 5.30–10pm. MAP P.53, POCKET MAP D13

The Black Diamond's upmarket waterfront restaurant is an immaculate, minimalist affair, with long beautifully dressed tables lined up along the quayside walkway. It's packed to the rafters throughout the day, with champagne and oysters (120kr) the lunchtime favourite, while the three-course evening menu, focused around local produce, will set you back 340kr. *Borgen* fans will notice that this is where many of PM Birgitte Nyborg's external meetings take place.

Nyhavn and Frederiksstad

Packed with busy bars and restaurants, canalside Nyhavn attracts thousands of visitors thanks to its pretty postcard setting. To its north are the elegant Rococo houses and immaculately straight streets of Frederiksstad, built as a grand symbol of Frederik V's reign. The huge dome of the Marmorkirken dominates the skyline, while three main north–south streets divide the area: Store Kongensgade, lined with galleries, restaurants and high-end shops; quieter Bredgade; and partially cobbled Amaliegade, which bisects the palaces of Amalienborg – the royals' official winter residence. All three streets lead up to Christian IV's impressive defensive fortress, the grass-bastioned Kastellet, close to which is a pair of inspirational museums. Finally, perched on a lonely rock off the Kastellet's northern edge, is the city's most famous icon – the diminutive Little Mermaid.

NYHAVN

MAP OPPOSITE, POCKET MAP E11–F11

Picturesque **Nyhavn** is perhaps the city's most popular tourist hangout. The "new harbour" was created in 1671 to link Kongens Nytorv to the sea – the earliest of the townhouses, no.9, dates from this period – and has been home to some famous residents – Hans Christian Andersen lived for a while at no.67. The area has not always been so salubrious, however: Nyhavn went through a long period as the city's most disreputable red-light district before its transformation into the welcoming visitor haunt of today. On a sunny summer's evening (there are outdoor heaters in winter) it's easy to see the attraction of sipping a beer while gazing over the historic yachts (usually) moored in the harbour. Be warned, though: food and drink does not come cheap.

NYHAVN

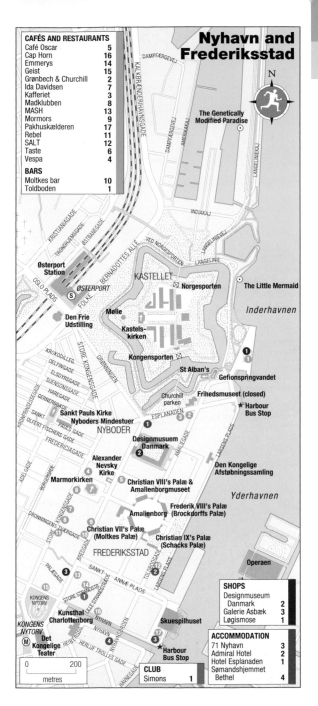

Nyhavn and Frederiksstad

CAFÉS AND RESTAURANTS

Café Oscar	5
Cap Horn	16
Emmerys	14
Geist	15
Grønbech & Churchill	2
Ida Davidsen	7
Kafferiet	3
Madklubben	8
MASH	13
Mormors	9
Pakhuskælderen	17
Rebel	11
SALT	12
Taste	6
Vespa	4

BARS

Moltkes bar	10
Toldboden	1

The Genetically
Modified Paradise

Østerport
Station

ØSTERPORT

KASTELLET

Norgesporten

The Little Mermaid

Inderhavnen

Den Frie
Udstilling

Mølle

Kastels-
kirken

Kongensporten

St Alban's

Gefionspringvandet

Churchill
parken

Frihedsmuseet (closed)

★ Harbour
Bus Stop

Sankt Pauls Kirke
Nyboders Mindestuer

NYBODER

ESPLANADEN

Designmusuem
Danmark

Den Kongelige
Afstøbningssamling

Alexander
Nevsky
Kirke

Marmorkirken

Christian VIII's Palæ &
Amalienborgmuseet

Yderhavnen

Frederik VIII's Palæ
Amalienborg (Brockdorffs Palæ)

Christian VII's Palæ
(Moltkes Palæ)

Christian IX's Palæ
(Schacks Palæ)

FREDERIKSSTAD

Operaen

KONGENS
NYTORV

KONGENS
NYTORV

Det
Kongelige
Teater

Kunsthal
Charlottenborg

Skuespilhuset

Harbour
Bus Stop

0   200
metres

SHOPS

Designmuseum Danmark	2
Galerie Asbæk	3
Løgismose	1

ACCOMMODATION

71 Nyhavn	3
Admiral Hotel	2
Hotel Esplanaden	1
Sømandshjemmet Bethel	4

CLUB

Simons	1

AMALIENBORG

KUNSTHAL CHARLOTTENBORG

Nyhavn 2 ⓦ kunsthalcharlottenborg
.dk. Tues & Thurs–Sun 11am–5pm, Wed
11am–8pm, 60kr. MAP P.59, POCKET MAP E11

Located between Kongens
Nytorv and Nyhavn (and with
entrances on both) the **Kunsthal
Charlottenborg** is housed in
one of the least prepossessing
palaces in Copenhagen. Built for
the illegitimate son of Frederik
III, it has since 1754 been home
to the Royal Danish Academy of
Fine Arts. There are no
permanent displays but
changing exhibitions of modern
art are put on in the newer
building (added in 1883)
behind. One such exhibition
in 1971, about the new hippie
movement, triggered the
founding of Christiania
(see p.80).

AMALIENBORG

MAP P.59, POCKET MAP F10

The winter residence of the
Danish royal family, **Amalienborg** is made up four almost
identical Rococo palaces,
arranged symmetrically around
an octagonal courtyard that
centres on a statue of Frederik
V on horseback. Designed by
royal architect Nicolai Eigtved

in 1750, the palaces were
originally built for (and funded
by) wealthy Danish nobles,
though the royals comman-
deered them following the
devastating fire at Christiansborg in 1794. Today all four
palaces are named both after
their original benefactor and a
subsequent resident royal. The
Queen lives in Christian IX's
Palæ – or Schacks Palæ – with
her husband Prince Henri,
while Frederik VIII's Palæ
(Brockdorffs Palæ) is home to
Crown Prince Frederik and
family; both are completely
off-limits.

You can however visit
Christian VIII's Palæ
(Levetzaus Palæ), the first floor
of which contains the
Amalienborgmuseet
(Amalienborg Museum; May–
Oct daily 10am–4pm, Nov–
April Tues–Sun 11am–4pm;
65kr; ⓦ amalienborgmuseet
.dk), devoted to more recent
royal history. The studies of
each of the last three kings have
been fully reconstructed
(complete with vast pipe
collections and family
portraits), giving a flavour of
their modern if by no means
luxurious lifestyles. It's also

possible to tour **Christian VII's Palæ** (Moltkes Palæ; July–Sept Sat & Sun 1pm & 2.30pm; 75kr), the Queen's guest residence, highlight of which is the fabulous Great Hall, considered one of the finest Rococo rooms in Europe.

Outside on the courtyard, the **changing of the guard** ceremony at noon each day is a great hit with kids. Childish souls may try to see if they can induce the bearskin-wearing guard to flinch – chances are they won't.

SKUESPILHUSET

Sankt Annæ Plads 36 ☎ 33 69 69 33, ⓦ kglteater.dk. Guided tours (75min) 100kr; check website for times. MAP P.59, POCKET MAP F11

Completed in 2008, the **Skuespilhuset** (Playhouse), around the corner from Nyhavn, is unanimously agreed to be one of the city's most elegant new buildings. It has a stunning position on the Inner Harbour, with a projecting upper storey that appears to be balancing precariously over the water's edge. A copper-clad tower thrusts skyward from within, while a wooden promenade encircles the building and doubles as an outdoor café. To see the inside, either join one of the irregular tours or take in a performance – though when purchasing tickets do check which venue it's being put on at.

MARMORKIRKEN

Frederiksgade 4 ☎ 33 15 01 44. Mon–Thurs & Sat 10am–5pm, Fri & Sun noon–5pm. Free. MAP P.59, POCKET MAP E10

Modelled on St Peter's in the Vatican, the **Marmorkirken** (Marble Church), also known as Frederikskirken, took almost 150 years to complete. Originally commissioned by Frederik V in 1749, the church's construction was halted twenty years later due to lack of funds, and only with financial support from a leading Danish industrial magnate, C.F. Tietgen, was it completed – using cheaper marble – in 1894, having languished in ruins for more than a century. Though the exterior is largely hidden behind scaffolding until 2017, you can still access the massive interior, dominated by a colossal **dome** some 31m in diameter. If you arrive at the right time (Aug daily 1pm & 3pm, Sept–July Sat & Sun 1pm & 3pm; 25kr), you can join a tour to climb the 260 steps to the top of the **dome**, from which there are spectacular views down over diminutive Copenhagen beneath you and towards the Swedish coastline in the distance. Note too how the relatively new Operaen across the harbour has been aligned perfectly with the Marmorkirken and Amalienborg.

MARMORKIRKEN INTERIOR

DESIGNMUSEUM DANMARK

Bredgade 68 ☎ 33 18 56 76,
🌐 designmuseum.dk. Tues & Thurs–Sun
11am–5pm, Wed 11am–9pm. 60kr. Tours
Sept–June Sun 2pm; free. MAP P.59.
POCKET MAP G6

DESIGN MUSEUM DENMARK

Formerly the Kunstindustrimuseet, and not to be confused with the Danish Design Center (see p.35), this temple to (predominantly Danish) design occupies the four wings of the old Frederiks Hospital. Pride of place among the permanent exhibitions goes to the section on twentieth-century **Danish applied art and craft**, which takes in the full range of the iconic designs that have given Denmark its international reputation – from Arne Jacobsen's Ant chair to Kaj Boyesen's classic wooden toy monkey and Ole Kirk Christiansen's Lego brick. Elsewhere, the collection traces the history of European and Asian applied and decorative art, with the emphasis on how it relates to the development of Danish design. The Asian collection is particularly strong – ranging from Japanese sword paraphernalia to Chinese Ming vases. Check out the selection in the museum shop (see p.64) if you fancy taking any pieces home with you.

The Danish Resistance

Despite pledging to remain neutral during World War II Denmark was occupied by German forces from April 9, 1940 until May 1945. While the occupation was not the bloodbath that unfurled elsewhere in Europe, **resistance groups** nonetheless sprung up, among them the "Churchill Club", a group of schoolboys who sabotaged German vehicles, and the Hvidsten Group (subject of a hit 2012 Danish film) who distributed British weapons from secret airdrops. One of the proudest moments of this period was the clandestine evacuation in October 1943 of the vast majority of Denmark's seven thousand Jews to safety in neutral Sweden; almost everyone seems to have an uncle or grandfather who was somehow involved.

Until recently the best place to get to grips with the Danish wartime experience was the **Frihedsmuseet** (Museum of Freedom, or Museum of Danish Resistance) at 7 Churchillparken. Sadly, on May 5, 2013, the museum was ravaged by fire – a tragedy attributed to arson. Fortunately, no archival records or artefacts – such as Himmler's eye patch, taken off him by the Allies as he was captured trying to flee in disguise – were lost in the blaze. At press time, no decisions had been made on when construction for a new museum building will begin. In the meantime the Ryvangen Memorial Park in Hellerup commemorates resistance fighters executed by the Nazis.

KASTELLET

Daily 6am–10pm. MAP P.59, POCKET MAP G5

Surrounded by grassy ramparts and a series of moats, Copenhagen's quaint **Kastellet** (Citadel) is one of the best-preserved star-shaped fortresses in northern Europe. Brainchild of Christian IV and completed by Frederik III, it was constructed to defend the city from all sides, including from the city itself in case of rebellion. Its terraced rows of immaculate, mansard-roofed barracks, painted in a warm red hues, are still occupied by troops, making this also one of Europe's oldest functioning military bases. The granite war memorial in its southwest corner, dedicated to the many Danish soldiers who have been lost in action around the world since 1948, was unveiled in 2011.

THE LITTLE MERMAID

MAP P.59, POCKET MAP G5

Sitting on a boulder in the Inner Harbour off the northern edge of Kastellet, looking forlornly out to sea, **The Little Mermaid** (*Den lille havfrue*) is the city's most famous symbol. The embodiment of Hans Christians Andersen's fairytale character, she was created by Danish sculptor Edvard Eriksen in 1913 and paid for by Carlsberg brewery magnate Carl Jakobsen. Considering her diminutive size and somewhat vacant facial expression, the cynical observer might find it difficult to fathom her appeal to the busloads of tourists that visit her 24 hours a day, though her tragic tale of doomed love for her dream prince still has a powerful hold on the Danish imagination. The statue has not had an easy life, either. She's been the frequent victim of radical groups, covered in paint several times and beheaded twice.

A more recent addition a few hundred metres to the north along the waterfront at Langeliniekaj, the Little Mermaid's iconoclastic "ugly sister" is far more entertaining. Part of Bjørn Nørgaard's sculpture garden **The Genetically Modified Paradise**, she sits like her older sister on a boulder in the water, but with body and limbs grotesquely elongated and contorted – perhaps a truer rendition of Andersen's Little Mermaid's suffering than the original statue.

THE LITTLE MERMAID

Shops

DESIGNMUSEUM DANMARK SHOP

Bredgade 68 ☎ 33 18 56 56,
Ⓦ designmuseum.dk. Tues & Thurs–Sun
11am–5pm, Wed 11am–9pm. MAP P.59,
POCKET MAP G6

The Design Museum's shop is a
great place for industrial
design, and to pick up
ceramics, glass, textiles and
jewellery, all Danish-made.
Check out Kaj Boyesen's
wooden animal toys and the
beautiful glassware by
Holmegaard.

GALERIE ASBÆK

Bredgade 23 ☎ 33 15 40 04, Ⓦ asbaek.dk.
Tues–Fri 11am–6pm, Sat 11am–4pm
MAP P.59, POCKET MAP E11

This well-known art gallery
sells works by some of the
country's leading contemporary
artists, including CoBrA
painter Carl Henning-Pedersen
(aka the "Scandinavian
Chagall") and photographer
Niels Bonde.

LØGISMOSE

Nordre Toldbod 16 ☎ 33 32 93 32,
Ⓦ loegismose.dk. Mon–Fri 10am–7pm, Sat
10am–5pm. MAP P.59, POCKET MAP G5

A cornucopia of fabulous wines
and spirits is on sale at this deli
on the Innerhavnen, as well as
delicious cheeses and
charcuterie from France, Spain
and Italy. It's also an outlet for
heavenly Summerbird
chocolate (see p.76).

Cafés and restaurants

CAFÉ OSCAR

Bredgade 58 ☎ 33 12 50 10, Ⓦ cafeoscar.dk.
Daily 9.30am–11pm. MAP P.59, POCKET MAP G6

Upmarket corner café a short
walk from Amalienborg,
serving a selection of excellent
smørrebrød (from 65kr),
burgers, sandwiches and salads,
plus a meat-focused evening
menu. Fabulous food aside, it's
to be seen hobnobbing with the
rich and famous that most
people come.

CAP HORN

Nyhavn 21 ☎ 33 12 85 04, Ⓦ caphorn.dk.
Daily 9am–midnight. MAP P.59, POCKET MAP E11

The best choice among the
long row of overpriced
restaurants along Nyhavns
Kanal, *Cap Horn* serves largely
organic fare, including juicy
burgers (129kr) and always
one or two seafood options
(from 189kr).

EMMERYS

Store Strandstræde 21 ☎ 33 93 01 33,
Ⓦ emmerys.dk. Mon–Fri 7.30am–6pm, Sat
8am–5pm. MAP P.59, POCKET MAP E11

Part of an ever-expanding
chain of café-bakeries,
Emmerys is famous for its
slow-risen organic bread,
which you sample in
sandwiches or as part of a
breakfast platter. It's a great
coffee stop, too, and treat
yourself to a superb gooey
brownie while you're at it.

CAP HORN

GRØNBECH & CHURCHILL

GEIST

Kongens Nytorv 8 ☎ 33 13 37 13,
🅦 restaurantgeist.dk. Daily noon–1am.
MAP P.59, POCKET MAP E11

This hip but unpretentious (and well-priced) spot is presided over by ex-*Paustian* chef Bo Bech. In the centre, the open kitchen has stools around it for diners' observation, while the thirty-dish menu focuses on some inventive fusions such as grilled octopus and strawberries (150kr) or vanilla ice cream, served with olives, cinnamon and liquorice (80kr).

GRØNBECH & CHURCHILL

Esplanaden 48 ☎ 32 21 32 30,
🅦 gronbech-churchill.dk. Mon–Fri
noon–2.30pm & 6pm–10pm, Sat 6pm–10pm
MAP P.59, POCKET MAP G6

Located across from Churchill-parken and the Frihedsmuseet (see box, p.62), this Michelin-starred restaurant pays homage to the British wartime leader. The evening menu is a choice of two four-course menus (both 500kr): the Grønbech menu, named after the head chef, typically lighter and healthier, and the Churchill "Juice and Power" menu leaning – fittingly enough – towards red meat (whisky and cigars optional).

There's also a vegetarian alternative (425kr), and at lunchtime a brace of daily changing two-course menus (275kr).

IDA DAVIDSEN

Store Kongensgade 70 ☎ 33 91 36 55,
🅦 idadavidsen.dk. Mon–Fri 10.30am–5pm.
MAP P.59, POCKET MAP E10

When the craving strikes for smørrebrød, it's to *Ida Davidsen* that the Danish royals decamp – and the elaborately assembled smørrebrød (from 65kr) and sandwiches are indeed fit for a king. *Dyrlægens natmad* (literally "vet's midnight snack" – buttered rye bread smeared with liver pate and topped with aspic and a slice of salted beef) and the prawn sandwich are particular highlights.

KAFFERIET

Esplanaden 44 ☎ 33 93 93 04, 🅦 kafferiet
.net. Mon–Fri 7.30am–6pm, Sat & Sun
10am–6pm. MAP P.59, POCKET MAP G6

Colourful and cosy little coffee shop across from Kastellet with a few tables inside and a couple outside on the street, too. There's delightful coffee and home-made cakes, plus interesting Italian confectionery: sweets from Pastiglie Leone and strong Amarelli licorice. A little gem in an otherwise café-barren area.

SALT

MADKLUBBEN

Store Kongensgade 66 ☎ 33 32 32 34,
Ⓦ madklubben.info. Mon–Sat 5.30pm–
midnight. MAP P.59, POCKET MAP E10
Branch of the wildly popular
restaurant chain that offers
simple, tasty food with fast and
efficient service (see p.93).

MASH

Bredgade 20 ☎ 33 13 93 00, Ⓦ mashsteak.
dk. Lunch Mon–Fri noon–3pm; dinner
Mon–Wed & Sun 5.30–10pm; Thurs–Sat
5.30–11pm. MAP P.59, POCKET MAP E11
MASH stands for Modern
American Steak House, which
is exactly what you get – juicy
steaks in a US diner setting.
Starters (110kr) range from
snails with garlic to half a
grilled lobster and the steaks
(from 265kr) come in all
shapes and sizes – from
Uruguayan tenderloin to
American bone-in ribeye, via
(Aussie-sourced) Wagyu filet.

MORMORS

Bredgade 45 ☎ 33 16 07 00, Ⓦ mormors.dk.
Mon–Fri 9.30am–4pm, Sat 11.30am–3pm.
MAP P.59, POCKET MAP E10
A homely pitstop, *Mormors*
("Grandma's") easily lives up to
its name with its warm and
welcoming feel. There's hot
soup for the cold winter
months (55kr), a range of

freshly made juices (42kr),
sandwiches galore and a
counter full of delicious cakes.
Park yourself in one of the
window seats inside, or at the
pavement tables out front.

PAKHUSKÆLDEREN

Nyhavn 71 ☎ 33 43 62 14, Ⓦ pakhuskaelderen
.com. Mon–Sat noon–midnight. MAP P.59,
POCKET MAP F11
Part of the grand *71 Nyhavn*
hotel overlooking Copenhagen's harbour, this stylish
gourmet restaurant features
plenty of exposed pine beams
and plenty of atmosphere.
Continental menu specialities
include braised pork cheek
with balsamico (110kr) or
breast of poularde with basil
and artichokes (230kr). Also
has a great bar open all day.

REBEL

Store Kongensgade 52 ☎ 33 32 32 09,
Ⓦ restaurantrebel.dk. Mon–Fri noon–4pm &
5.45pm–midnight, Sat 5.45pm–midnight.
MAP P.59, POCKET MAP E10
Compact restaurant spread
over two floors serving elegant
French-inspired tapas. It's
especially renowned for its beef
tartare, served with rhubarb,
herbed mayonnaise and
vinaigrette, and turbot served
with escargot, lobster glaze and
tarragon. Two dishes 269kr.

SALT

Toldbodgade 24 ☎ 33 74 14 44, ⓦ saltrestaurant.dk. Daily noon to 4pm & 5–10.30pm. MAP P.59, POCKET MAP F11

Hotel Admiral's characterful restaurant has seating both in the charming wood-beamed interior and out on the waterfront. The excellent seafood menu (from 315kr for two courses) and the mouthwatering selection of Nordic cheeses (95kr) can hardly be bettered.

TASTE

Store Kongensgade 80–82 ☎ 33 93 77 97, ⓦ tastedeli.eu. Mon–Wed 9.30am–6pm, Thurs & Fri 9.30am–7pm, Sat & Sun 10am–6pm. MAP P.59, POCKET MAP E10

This fabulous deli (with a few tables out front) serves gorgeous home-made salads, sandwiches plus a range of exquisite cakes – though as everything is of tip-top quality nothing comes cheap. Try the grilled goats' cheese, beetroot and walnut sandwich, with a honey and rosemary dressing (78kr).

VESPA

Store Kongensgade 90 ☎ 33 11 37 00, ⓦ cofoco.dk. Mon–Sat 5.30pm–midnight. MAP P.59, POCKET MAP F6

Part of the Cofoco "food empire", which follows a simple no-frills concept. What's on offer is a well-prepared four-course Italian set menu for 250kr. Restrictive perhaps, but excellent value for money.

Bars

MOLTKES BAR

Dronningens Tværgade 2 ☎ 33 15 91 06, ⓦ moltkes.com. Fri & Sat 6pm–2am. MAP P.59, POCKET MAP E10

With speakeasy references back to New York in the 1920s, this time-warped cocktail bar – next door to Amalienborg in a court official's mansion – serves all of the well-known classics as well as a few forgotten ones.

TOLDBODEN

Nordre Toldbod 24 ☎ 33 93 07 60, ⓦ toldboden.com. Daily 11am–10pm, plus Sat 10pm–4am. MAP P.59, POCKET MAP G5

With great views of the Inner Harbour, *Tolboden* has few rivals for the title of the Copenhagen's most stunningly located bar. It's a great place for drinks during the week, particularly in summer when you can chill out in the deckchairs. On Saturdays it transforms into a heaving nightclub.

Club

SIMONS

Store Strandstræde 14 ☎ 53 38 90 03, ⓦ simonscopenhagen.com. Fri & Sat 10pm–4am. MAP P.59, POCKET MAP E11

Trendy nightclub housed in a former art gallery, which requires you to register via their website in order to get in. The door policy is notoriously strict, especially on Saturdays. Expect dwarf bartenders and wild nights.

Rosenborg and around

Christian IV's Renaissance summer palace, the Rosenborg Slot, provides a regal contrast with the crowded streets of the inner city to the east. To its west, running from Østerport station in the north to Vesterport in the south is an almost continuous string of attractive parks and gardens. Apart from being lovely places to explore, they also house a couple of significant art museums: the Statens Museum for Kunst and Hirschsprungske Samling, and the city's Botanical Gardens. It was thanks to visionary Town Planner Ferdinand Mekdahl that the ring of ramparts and bastions encircling the city here were maintained as a green belt in 1857. The area between the ramparts and the lake later developed into sought-after residential areas and streets such as Nansensgade have a strong neighbourhood feel.

ROSENBORG SLOT

4A Østervoldgade ☎ 33 15 32 86.
ⓦ rosenborgslot.dk. Castle: May, Sept & Oct
daily 10am–4pm; June–Aug daily 10am–5pm;
Nov–April Tues–Sun 11am–2pm. 80kr, 110kr
for combined ticket with Amalienborg.
Gardens: sunrise to sunset; free.
MAP PP.70–71, POCKET MAP E6

A Disney-esque fairytale palace, the **Rosenborg Slot** was originally built as a summer residence for Christian IV, a retreat from the rabble at Christiansborg. Completed in 1634, it's a grand red-brick Renaissance edifice decorated with spires and towers and ornate Dutch gables. The palace remained a royal residence until 1838, when it was opened to the public.

The star exhibit inside is the **crown jewels,** chief among them the Crown of the Absolute Monarch which weighs in at a

Park life

Based around the Rosenborg Slot, the beautifully manicured **Kongens Have** (King's Garden) is Copenhagen's oldest park and a favoured spot in summer when there is live music and performances in the puppet theatre (June–Aug daily except Mon 2 & 3pm; free; Ⓦmarionetteatret.dk). Stretching north from the Botanical Gardens, the undulating hills of **Østre Anlæg** are part of the old fortifications and house a number of different children's playgrounds including one in front of the National Museum of Art. **Ørstedsparken**, with its rolling hills and rampart lake, is a popular place to go in winter for skating and downhill sledging. There are also two innovative playgrounds here, one with staff at hand to show you the ropes. Come nightfall it becomes a gay hangout (in case you were wondering about the signs promoting safe sex).

hefty two kilos and sports two massive sapphires. The jewels are kept locked in the basement Treasury, behind thick steel doors. Also downstairs are the priceless wines of the Royal cellar, only cracked open at very special occasions. Before heading down here it's worth taking in Frederik III's lavish marble room with its extravagant stucco ceiling and a chess set made up of Danish and Swedish pieces (in reference to the war he lost to Karl Gustav in 1658). Another highlight of the palace is the magnificent **Long Hall** on the second floor with its gilded coronation throne, made from narwhal tusk, and three silver lions standing guard.

BOTANISK HAVE

Gothersgade 130 Ⓦ botanik.snm.ku.dk May–Sept 8.30am–6pm, Oct–April Tues–Sun 8.30am–4pm MAP PP70–71, POCKET MAP E6

Relocated in 1874 from a small park behind Charlottenborg palace (p.60) the **Botanisk Have** (Botanical Gardens) packs in pretty much every plant you'll find in Denmark together with several exotic species. It's a pleasant and peaceful place to wander, with its long squiggly pond clearly showing the area's previous incarnation as the city ramparts. Among the many greenhouses in the gardens, the grand Palm House overshadows them all. It was donated by brewing magnate Carl Jacobsen who was deeply involved in its design and various ingenious temperature and humidity controls. You will also find houses for cacti, orchids, alpine plants, and a new greenhouse for endangered species (check the website for their specific opening times).

The Botanical Museum part of the gardens is currently closed. A brand new National Natural History Museum, complete with innovative underground architecture, is due to open in 2017 at the northern end of the gardens.

Rosenborg and around

CAFÉS AND RESTAURANTS	
Aamanns	2
Bankerât	15
BioM	3
Café and Ølhalle	5
Firefly	8
Koefoed	16
La Rocca	6
Nice	14
Orangeriet	4
Pintxos	9
Torvehallerne	12
Sticks N Sushi	10
Un Mercato	11

BARS	
Bibendum	13
Café Globen	17
Kalaset	7
Kruts Karport	1

ACCOMMODATION	
Generator	3
Ibsen	1
Jørgensen	2

SHOPS	
Keramik og Glasværkstedet	1
Pegasus	2
Tranquebar	3

VENUE	
Culture Box	1

STATENS MUSEUM FOR KUNST

Sølvgade 48–50 ☎ 33 74 84 94, ⓦ smk.dk.
Tues & Thurs–Sun 10am–5pm, Wed
10am–8pm. Permanent exhibition free,
changing exhibit 95kr MAP ABOVE, POCKET MAP E5

Found in the southeastern corner of Østre Anlæg park, the vast **Statens Museum for Kunst** (National Museum of Art) houses the bulk of Christian II's extensive collection of European paintings and sculptures. Housed in an 1896 building by Dahlerup (see also Ny Carlsberg Glyptotek, p.34) and complemented by a modern extension in 1998, the collection is divided into European art from the fourteenth to the eighteenth century, Danish and Nordic Art from 1750 to 1900, French art from 1900–1930, and modern art from the twentieth century. Trying to see it all in one day is almost impossible. Instead, if you're interested in Danish art, head straight for the second floor where works from the so-called Golden Age – the nineteenth century – are displayed in largely chronologically order. Look out especially for the beautifully lit paintings of the Skagen school – among

STATENS MUSEUM FOR KUNST

them P.S. Krøyer and Anna Ancher. Look out too for the stark almost photographic scenes of Copenhagen in the nineteenth century by Vilhelm Hammershøi. On the second floor you'll also find work from the twentieth-century CoBrA movement (a collection of artists from Copenhagen, Brussels and Amsterdam). Contemporary international art is displayed in the museum's new extension. Recent temporary exhibits have included Matisse and Miro.

HIRSCHSPRUNGSKE SAMLING

Stockholmsgade 20 ☎35 42 03 36, ⊕hirschsprung.dk. Tues–Sun 11am–4pm. 75kr, free Wed. MAP ABOVE, POCKET MAP F5

More manageable than the Statens Museum, the **Hirschprung Collection** focuses on art from the Danish Golden Age (1800–1850),

donated by Heinrich Hirschsprung, a second-generation German Jew who had made his fortune in tobacco. Housed in a beautiful Neoclassical pavilion, paintings are displayed in small intimate rooms (a condition Hirschsprung set before handing over his collection to the state). As at the Staten Museum, the work of the Skagens artists P.S. Krøyer and Anna Ancher particularly stands out. Tranquil bucolic landscapes by P.C. Skovgaard and Johan Lundbye are also worth noting. More entertaining are the gossip-magazine-like paintings by Kristians Zahrtmann who depicted eighteenth-century royal scandals such as English-born Queen Caroline Mathilde's affair with court physician Johann Friedrich Struensee.

71

ARBEJDERMUSEET

Rømersgade 22 ☎ 33 93 25 75.
🌐 arbejdermuseet.dk. Daily 10am–4pm, 65kr.
MAP PP.70–71, POCKET MAP A10

Dedicated to the Danish workers movement, **Arbejder-museet** is housed in the group's old meeting house from 1878 and covers the cultural history of the Danish working class from 1850 onwards. Although it's probably more of interest to Danes, the historic assembly hall is worth a peek. Its tranquil bucolic decor witnessed some of the movement's most significant gatherings, not least the Socialist World Congress of 1910 which had Lenin himself in attendance (there's a Russian-made statue of him in the foyer dating from the late 1980s). The children's section, although mostly in Danish, is also popular, and often noisy, featuring doll's houses, dressing-up gear, colouring-in books and even a small pretend brewery. There's also a museum shop selling iconic workers' posters from the old Soviet Union and a basement restaurant (p.75) knocking out traditional workers' dishes from the last century.

DAVIDS SAMLING

Kronprinsessegade 30 ☎ 33 73 49 49.
🌐 davidmus.dk. Tues & Fri 1–5pm, Wed 10am–9pm, Thurs 10am–5pm, Sat & Sun 11am–5pm. Free. MAP PP.70–71, POCKET MAP D10

Spread over all five floors of an eighteenth-century apartment building, **Davids Samling** comprises the remarkable collection of one C.L. David (1878–1960), a Danish lawyer who devoted his

Dining with the Danes

Danish food exploded on the global stage in 2010, when *Noma* was named the world's top restaurant. Since then, simple Nordic dishes made from seasonal, locally sourced ingredients (preferably foraged from the nearest hedge) have taken Copenhagen by storm, with many new restaurants riding the waves of *Noma's* fame. In 2013, while *Noma* dropped down to no.2 in the world, the Danish capital was awarded a total of fifteen Michelin stars – more than Stockholm, Oslo and Helsinki put together. Fortunately it's still possible to sate your craving for scrumptious Scandi cuisine without killing your bank balance –try *Atlas Bar* (p.46), *Royal Café* (p.49) and *Morgenstedet* (p.84). Alternatively head straight to the Torvehaller food market (p.76) to shop where the chefs shop.

NYBODER

new **Torvehallerne** food market (see p.76) has been a resounding success, attracting over sixty thousand visitors a week to its artisan stalls and restaurants. **Israels Plads** square next door, traditionally known for its flower stalls, is undergoing major rejuvenation, too. Its completion is planned to coincide with the opening of the new enhanced Nørreport Metro station in 2017 when it will – according to the team of architects – appear as a flying carpet with various water features. The square was given its current name in 1968 in memory of Jewish persecution in Denmark during World War II.

life to the acquisition of fine and applied art. It's a labyrinth of rooms, and the museum plan handed out on arrival will prove essential. The highlight without doubt is the extensive exhibition of Islamic art on the third and fourth floors. One of the most important in the West, it includes delicate Persian miniatures, striking blue Ottoman mosaics and beautifully decorated glass bowls from Egypt and Syria. David's collections of eighteenth- and nineteenth-century porcelain and furniture and twentieth-century art (look out for the evocative landscape paintings by Vilhelm Hammershøi and the extravagant French ceramics) are also impressive but don't match the heights of the Islamic finds.

TORVEHALLERNE AND ISRAELS PLADS

Market halls: Frederiksborggade 21
ⓦ torvehallernekbh.dk. Mon–Thurs 10am–7pm, Fri 10am–8pm, Sat 10am–6pm, Sun 11am–5pm. MAP PP.70–71, POCKET MAP B10
Since its opening in 2011, the

NYBODER

Nyboder Mindestuer, 24 Sankt Paulsgade
ⓣ 20 99 42 29, ⓦ nybodersmindestuer.dk. Sun 11am–2pm. 15kr. MAP PP.70–71, POCKET MAP F6.
Standing out in contrast to the area's grand regal mansions, the colourful and quaint **Nyboder** district is made up of a series of rows of cute, predominantly ochre-coloured terraced houses. The area was originally built in the 1630s to provide housing for Christian IV's ever-expanding naval fleet, though most of the current buildings date from the eighteenth century – all except for a single row of houses along Sankt Paulsgade, where the **Nyboders Mindestuer** (Nyboder Memorial Rooms) has been largely kept intact and functions as a museum. Diminutive though Nyboder's houses may be, this has always been a sought-after place to live, with its own private school and hospital, and demand remains high, particularly since (as of 2006) priority is no longer given to military personnel.

Shops

KERAMIK OG GLASVÆRKSTEDET

Kronprinsessegade 43 ☎ 33 32 89 91,
ⓦ keramikogglasvaerkstedet.dk. Wed–Fri
noon to 6pm, Sat 11am–2pm. MAP PP.70–71,
POCKET MAP F6

Funky workshop-cum-gallery
selling delicate and minimalist
ceramics and glassware made
on the premises by four
independent artists.

PEGASUS

Nørre Farimagsgade 53 ☎ 33 32 56 50,
ⓦ pegasus.dk. Mon–Fri 2.30–6pm.
MAP PP.70–71, POCKET MAP A10

Nerdy basement store selling a
huge selection of comics and
graphic novels (new and
secondhand) from around the
globe with an especially good
selection of American comics.

TRANQUEBAR

Borgergade 14 ☎ 33 12 55 12, ⓦ tranquebar
.net. Mon–Thurs 10am–6pm, Fri 10am–11pm,
Sat 10am–3pm. MAP PP.70–71, POCKET MAP E10

Well-stocked book and music
shop with a vast selection of
travel literature and world
music (and, of course, a good
range of Rough Guides). The
bookstore café sells lunch
platters (noon to 3pm) from
Koefoed (see opposite), up
the road.

Cafés and restaurants

AAMANNS

Øster Farimagsgade 10 ☎ 35 55 33 44,
ⓦ aamanns.dk. Restaurant: Wed–Sat noon to
4pm & 6–11pm, Sun noon–4pm; take out:
Mon–Fri 10.30am–8pm, Sat 11am–4.30pm,
Sun noon–4.30pm. MAP PP.70–71, POCKET MAP E5

This stylish ode to traditional
Danish open sandwiches makes
hands-down the city's best

AAMANNS

smørrebrød. Head chef Adam
Aamanns ensures everything is
free range and sourced from
local Danish farmers (3-course
menu 315kr). It's perfect for a
visit with children, too, who
love the bite-sized portions.
You can either eat in or take
out in smart little picnic-
friendly boxes.

BANKERÅT

Ahlefeldtsgade 27–29 ☎ 33 93 69 88,
ⓦ bankeraat.dk. Mon–Fri 9.30am to midnight,
Sat & Sun 10.30am to midnight. MAP PP.70–71,
POCKET MAP A10

Oldie but goodie Nansensgade
café which is just as popular
now as when it opened in the
80s with its largely unchanged
quirky décor. Its signature
breakfast/brunch Morgenkom-
plex comes in lots of different
variations including "Full
Engelsk". Turns into a popular
bar come evening.

BIOM

Fredericiagade 78 ☎ 33 32 24 66, ⓦ biom.dk.
Tues–Sat 11.30am–11pm; Brunch Sat & Sun
10am–2pm. MAP PP.70–71, POCKET MAP F6

Cool organic restaurant
offering a good range of

vegetarian options and a few tasty meaty ones, too. If in doubt try the lunchtime mushroom risotto (95kr).

CAFE AND ØLHALLE

Rømersgade 22 🌐 arbejdermuseet.dk. Daily 11am–5pm. MAP PP.70–71, POCKET MAP B10

You may find the traditional nineteenth-century worker's fare served here a little heavy, but it is authentic and very tasty. Try the *Dagens Husmandsret* (daily special) for 99kr, or the *Bondekonens stegte sild* (farmer's wife's fried herring) for 78kr. Also on the menu are some old-school desserts.

FIREFLY

Frederiksborggade 26 ☎ 33 36 33 30, 🌐 fireflygarden.com. Mon–Sat 11.30am–10pm. MAP PP.70–71, POCKET MAP B10

Describing itself as a botanic restaurant, *Firefly* makes weird and wonderful vegetarian, vegan and raw combos such as spelt risotto served with quinoa, capers, cream and mushrooms (115kr). They also serve excellent smoothies and organic cocktails and wines.

LA ROCCA

KOEFOED

Landgreven 3 ☎ 56 48 22 24, 🌐 restaurant-koefoed.dk. Tues–Sat noon–3pm & 5.30–10pm. MAP PP.70–71, POCKET MAP E10

Elegant *Koefoed* is an ode to the gourmet island of Bornholm, famous for its slow-food ethos and quality produce. The lunchtime smørrebrød (from 75kr) has won awards, while the short dinner menu starts at 195kr for a main (Bornholmer rooster or cod with oysters, for example). Eat in the atmospheric, vaulted, stone-walled interior or outside at one of the streetside tables.

LA ROCCA

Vendersgade 23-25 ☎ 33 12 66 55, 🌐 larocca.dk. Daily noon–10.30pm. MAP PP.70–71, POCKET MAP A10

Classical Italian restaurant at *Ibsens Hotel*, offering refined Italian dining such as a fine mixed seafood grill (245kr) and a couple of good pizzas, too.

NICE

Nansensgade 66 ☎ 33 12 10 22, 🌐 cafenice .dk. Mon–Thurs & Sun 11am–11pm, Fri & Sat 10am to midnight. MAP PP.70–71, POCKET MAP A10.

Small, ramshackle basement café-restaurant seemingly transplanted from Paris, producing outstanding steak (179kr) and *moules frites* (150kr).

ORANGERIET

Kronprinsessegade 13 ☎ 33 11 13 07, 🌐 restaurant-orangeriet.dk. Mon–Sat 11.30am to midnight. Sun noon to 4pm. MAP PP.70–71, POCKET MAP D10

Atmospheric glass-encased café-restaurant located along the western wall of Kongens Have, with great views of the gardens, serving excellent smørrebrød for lunch and more substantial meals for dinner starting at 185kr for grilled skate with cauliflower puree.

A taste of Torvehallerne

A few of Torvehallerne's best stalls are listed below and should be visited in their own right:

Unika (stall E4) – retail outlet for cheeses usually only sold to Michelin-starred restaurants.

360 degrees north (stall E2) – outlet for small artisanal food producers from around the country

The Coffee Collective (stall C1) – the best coffee in town

Hallernes Smørrebrød (stall F2) – great smørrebrød selected from a large display cabinet; Mikkeller on draught.

Gorms Pizza (stall G1) – freshly made pizza from a wood-fired oven

Tapa del Torro (stall F10) – delicious home-made tapas

Summerbird (stall A3) – chocolate made in heaven

TORVEHALLERNE

PINTXOS

Nansensgade 63 ☎ 33 93 66 55, ⓦ pintxostapas.dk. Mon–Sat 5–11pm. MAP PP.70–71, POCKET MAP A10

Genuine Spanish restaurant with genuine Spanish waiters, and tapas galore (from 49kr) in a romantic courtyard.

TORVEHALLERNE

Frederiksborggade 21 ⓦ torvehallernekbh.dk. Mon–Thurs 10am–7pm, Fri 10am–8pm, Sat 10am–6pm, Sun 11am–5pm. Coffee and freshly baked bread available Mon–Sat from 8am, Sun from 9am. Restaurants and take-outs stay open an hour later than the market. MAP PP.70–71, POCKET MAP B10

Denmark's biggest and best food market. It's split into two long open-sided halls, one featuring meat, cheese and fish and a non-smelly section where you'll find chocolate, bread and the like. In between are plenty of outdoor benches at which to eat. A great way to explore Torvehallerne is to join the city's new Food Tours (box, p.131).

STICKS'N'SUSHI

Nansensgade 59 ☎ 33 11 14 07, ⓦ sushi.dk. Mon–Thurs & Sun 10am–11pm, Fri & Sat 10am–11.30pm. MAP PP.70–71, POCKET MAP A10

Copenhagen's original purveyors of raw fish to the masses. Starting out some twenty years ago, they now have branches across the city (and one in London). They can still make a mean sushi and also specialize in yakitori sticks (marinated skewers of meat and fish) as well as an outstanding array of salads, best of which is the scrumptious fish-bowl salad (144kr).

UN MERCATO

Torvehallerne, Frederiksborggade 21.
Mon–Fri 10am–9pm, Sat 10am–8pm, Sun
11am–8pm. MAP PP.70–71.
POCKET MAP B10

No-nonsense Italian rotisserie
on the first floor of Torvehallerne, run by the people
behind *Cofoco* restaurants.
The lunchtime flame-grilled
chicken or porchetta
sandwiches (65kr) are
mouthwatering – even just
writing about them.

Bars

BIBENDUM

Nansensgade 45 ☎ 33 33 07 74, ⓦ bibendum
.dk. Mon–Sat 4pm–midnight. MAP PP.70–71,
POCKET MAP A10

Small cosy basement winebar
with a huge selection of wine,
all of which are sold by
the glass as well as by the
bottle. Also good nibbles (all
costing 87kr) to soak up the
alcohol such as cheese and
charcuterie platters and a
delicious fish soup.

CAFÉ GLOBEN

Turesensgade 2b ☎ 33 93 00 77,
ⓦ cafegloben.dk. Mon–Thurs 5–10pm, Fri
4pm–1am. MAP PP.70–71, POCKET MAP A11

Laid-back travellers' haunt
halfway between a club and a
café with lots of guidebooks
lying around and people keen
to talk about their latest
adventures. Selling a good
range of brews from home and
abroad, they don't mind if you
bring your own food and eat at
their tables.

KALASET

Vendersgade 16 ☎ 33 33 00 35. Mon–Thurs
10am–midnight, Fri & Sat 10am–2am, Sun
10am–11pm. MAP PP.70–71, POCKET MAP A10

Quirky shabby chic basement
café which spills out onto the

pavement during summer when
it's an excellent spot to catch a
couple of rays while sipping a
cool drink. During weekends a
DJ gets the party going.

KRUTS KARPORT

Øster Farimagsgade 12 ☎ 35 26 86 38.
Mon–Thurs noon to midnight, Fri & Sat
noon–2am, Sun 2–7pm. MAP PP.70–71,
POCKET MAP E5

Copenhagen's first French-style
café, *Kruts Karport* stocks the
city's largest selection of
whisky, and is one of the few
places you can order an
absinthe. That said, the
selection of foreign draught
beer is not bad either.

Venues

CULTURE BOX

Kronprinsessegade 54 ☎ 33 32 50 50,
ⓦ culture-box.dk. Fri & Sat midnight to 6am.
MAP PP.70–71, POCKET MAP F6

Spread over two floors, with a
Berlin-style industrial decor,
this popular bar-club keeps
going until the wee hours of
the morning. Revellers tend to
get the party started at *The
Cocktail Box* bar next door.

BIBENDUM

Christianshavn and around

With its tight network of narrow canals and cobbled streets, the island of Christianshavn – sometimes known as Little Amsterdam – is one of the city's most charming areas. Water is omnipresent, perhaps not surprising given the area's origins – the island was constructed from reclaimed land in the sixteenth century to form a defensive arc around the city. For the most part the attractions here are low-key, though Christianshavn's principal source of tourist intrigue – the unique "Freetown" of Christiania, home to one of the world's most famous alternative communities – pulls in almost a million visitors a year. To its north, the former naval island of Holmen is home to the city's impressive new opera house, while to the south the industrial Islands Brygge quay, stretching along the harbourfront of Amager, has been reenergized with a funky waterside park and lively cultural centre, as well as Copenhagen's most exclusive new residential area.

CHRISTIANSHAVNS KANAL

MAP OPPOSITE, POCKET MAP E14–F14

Lined on both sides by cobbled streets and colourful merchant's houses, the tranquil **Christianshavns Kanal** originally provided the main way of accessing the island. This picturesque area is redolent of old Amsterdam, and indeed was designed by a Dutch architect, Johan Semp, who was commissioned in the early seventeenth century by Christian IV to plan the district.

Then as now, Christianshavn's main square, **Christianshavn Torv**, was the focal point of public transport to the island – today there's a metro station (underground) and constant flow of buses, as well as a canal-boat stop. A notable exception to the imposing historic buildings around the square is the Modernist **Lagkagehuset** (Layercake House) at Torvegade 45. It created riotous debate when it was built in 1931 as it was felt it didn't blend in to its historic surroundings but today is deemed a national treasure.

CAFÉS AND RESTAURANTS
Café Oven Vande 7
Christianshavns
 Bådudlejning 9
DAC Café 6
Kadeau 12
Kaffesyndikatet 8
Lagkagehuset 10
Morgenstedet 3
Noma 2
Nose Wise 14
Spicey Kitchen Café 11
Spiseloppen 5
Viva 13

BARS
Halvandet 1
Nemoland 4

VENUES
Islands Brygges Kulturhus 2
Loppen 1

SHOPS
Christiania Cykler 2
DAC Bookshop 3
Nordatlantens Brygge 1

ACCOMMODATION
CPH Living 1

Christianshavn and around

CHRISTIANS KIRKE

Strandgade 1 🌐 christianskirke.com.
Tues–Fri 10am–4pm. MAP P.79, POCKET MAP E14

Boxed in between a quartet of elegant sandstone-and-copper-clad office buildings designed by Henning Larsen on one side and a set of apartment blocks on the other, the Rococo **Christians Kirke** (1759) looks oddly out of place. Designed by Nicolai Eigtved (also known for Amalienborg Slot), it was originally built for the city's German congregation and still functions as a church, though thanks to its theatre-like interior – with a central pulpit and three-storeyed gallery – is nowadays best known (to visitors at least) as a music and arts venue, particularly during the annual jazz festival (see p.134).

VOR FRELSERSKIRKE

Skt Annæ Gade 29 ☎ 32 54 68 83, 🌐 www
.vorfrelserskirke.dk. Church: daily
11am–3.30pm; free. Tower: June–mid-Sept
daily 10am–7.30pm, mid-Sept–May daily
10am–4pm (Sun opens at 10.30am); 35kr.
MAP P.79, POCKET MAP F13

Capped by an iconic church tower, its soaring spire wrapped in a gilded spiral external staircase which culminates in a globe carrying a flag-waving Jesus, **Vor Frelserskirke** (Our Saviour's Church) is an unmissable feature of the Christianshavn skyline. Constructed in the late 1600s, the church owes its opulence to Christian V, whose status as Denmark's first absolute monarch is underlined by some lavish Baroque flourishes. Inside, look out especially for the two stucco elephants holding up the gigantic three-storey organ, though the real highlight is the ascent of the **tower**, accessed by a separate entrance. There are 400 steps to the top, 150 of which are external – quite a challenge on a busy summer's day – but the stupendous views across the city are ample reward.

CHRISTIANIA

Main entrance on Prinsessegade.
Infocaféen daily noon–6pm. Guided tours
(starting at the main entrance) Sat & Sun
3pm; 40kr. MAP P.79, POCKET MAP G8

A self-proclaimed autonomous enclave with its own govern-ance and rules, **Freetown Christiania** is Copenhagen's main alternative claim to fame. Ever since 1971, when a group of homeless Copenhageners

"Christiania will never die"

Ever since its inception more than forty years ago, residents have struggled to defend Christiania's existence. Clashes over the residents' occupation (for free) of prime city real estate, past non-payment of taxes, and – most frequently – with police over the drug trade have been legion. Each time however Christiania has survived. The future looked bleak in early 2011, when the government's intentions to redevelop the area forced the community to close altogether, though later that year a remarkable deal was brokered allowing Christiania to buy the buildings that the government wishes to sell at sub-market rates (still a cool 76 million kroner), and to pay annual rent of 6 million kroner for the rest. To fund its survival, the community has issued so-called People's Shares (🌐 christianiafolkeaktie .dk) in the hope that outside supporters will provide help.

MURAL, CHRISTIANIA

first occupied the disused Bådsmandsstræde army barracks, Christiania has attracted controversy, its very existence perennially threatened (see box, opposite). Today, thanks in no small part to its open cannabis trade, it's one of the city's most visited tourist attractions. Despite its dishevelled look and whacked-out feel – it can be an intimidating place to explore, not least because of the many dogs running around – it's a remarkable place. Egalitarian, creative and ecologically minded, the ideals of its thousand-or-so residents have resulted in some truly unique self-built homes, imaginative businesses, and a host of flourishing artistic venues.

Extending for around 1km along the bastions that straddle Christian IV's picturesque defensive moat, there is quite a lot of Christiania to see, and the best way to experience it is either to join one of the immensely informative (if inevitably one-sided) guided tours, or buy a copy of the *Christiania Guide* (20kr) from the Infocaféen, in the **Loppebygningen** building to the left of the main entrance. Housed within the same building, a former artillery magazine, are the **Gallopperiet** art gallery (ⓦgallopperiet.dk), *Spiseloppen* restaurant (see p.85) and Loppen music venue (see p.85).

Continuing along the main artery, you reach **Carl Madsens Plads**, lined with stalls selling knick-knacks and fast food, which marks the beginning of **Pusherstreet** – impossible to miss from its unmistakable aroma. Lining the street are rows of well-stocked shacks selling everything from pre-rolled joints to smoking paraphernalia. A couple of basic rules apply on Pusher-street: don't run (or the stallholders will think there's a police raid) and don't take photos. Also remember that the use of hash is still a criminal offence in Denmark.

Following the edge of the moat around *Nemoland* (see p.85) leads you into the quieter, greener and more residential area. Here you will find some of Christiania's most ingenious alternative dwellings. A pedestrian bridge crosses the moat at the next bastion, or you can continue along past four bastions to the public road at the end, and follow the moat path back on the opposite side.

DANSK ARKITEKTUR CENTER

Strandgade 27B ☎ 32 57 19 30, ⓦ dac.dk. Mon–Fri 10am–6pm, Wed until 9pm, Sat & Sun 10am–5pm. Exhibition 40kr. Architectural tours May–Sept Sun 11am; 75kr; bike hire not included. MAP P.79, POCKET MAP F13

Housed in a beautifully restored warehouse building on the waterfront next to the former naval dry dock (the most advanced of its kind when constructed in the sixteenth century), the **Danish Architecture Centre** hosts changing exhibitions of new Danish and international architecture, has a well-stocked bookshop (see opposite), and a first-floor café with perhaps the best views in town (see opposite). In summer the centre organizes weekly **tours** on foot or by bike to an area of Copenhagen of particular interest to fans of new architecture – typically to Ørestaden, Holmen or along the harbourfront; book in advance on the website.

OPERAEN

Holmen ☎ 33 69 69 69, ⓦ operaen.dk. Tours most Sat & Sun; 100kr. Harbour Bus. MAP P.79, POCKET MAP G6

Occupying a prominent position on the compact island of Holmen diametrically across the water from the Marmorkirken, the Henning Larsen-designed **Operaen** (Opera House) is visible from almost any point along the harbour. It's a striking building, surmounted by an enormous flat roof that delicately overhangs the water's edge, while the no-expense-spared interior features gigantic outlandish lighting globes, designed by Danish-Icelandic artist Oluf Eliasson, in the foyer; note too the Jura sandstone walls inset with masses of tiny fossils. To gain access, though, you'll need

OPERAEN

either to see a performance (doors open 2hr beforehand) or join a guided tour.

ISLANDS BRYGGE

MAP P.79, POCKET MAP F9

Just south of Christianshavn, on the island of Amager, the Islands Brygge development is fast becoming one of the city's most happening areas. Much of this former industrial harbour strip has been converted into a waterfront park, the **Havneparken** – popular with people from all walks of life, from parents with prams to parkour enthusiasts – with cultural activity focused around the Islands Brygges Kulturhus (see p.85). Best of all however is the innovative, council-run **harbour pool** (June–Aug Mon–Fri 7am–7pm, Sat & Sun 9am–7pm; free), the perfect place to cool off on hot summer days.

The quayside walkway extends all the way south to the sleek bicycle and pedestrian bridge, officially the **Bryggebroen** ("Quay bridge"), which gives access across to Fisketorvet and Vesterbro.

Shops

CHRISTIANIA CYKLER

Mælkeven 83A, Christiania ☎ 32 54 87 48, ⓦ christianiabikes.dk. Mon–Fri 9am–5pm, Sat 10am–2pm. MAP P.79, POCKET MAP G8

Classic, sturdy and super-cool, Christiania Bikes' handcrafted three-wheel cargo cycles are one of the city's icons. Prices start at 9,500kr.

DAC BOOKSHOP

Strandgade 27B ☎ 32 57 19 30, ⓦ dac-bookshop.dk. Mon–Fri 10am–6pm, Wed till 9pm, Sat & Sun 10am–5pm. MAP P.79, POCKET MAP F13

The Danish Architecture Centre's attractive bookshop stocks just about every title on modern architecture you could ever wish for.

NORDATLANTENS BRYGGE

Strandgade 91 ☎ 32 83 37 00, ⓦ bryggen.dk. Mon–Fri 10am–5pm, Sat & Sun noon–5pm. MAP P.79, POCKET MAP G7

Housed in an enormous eighteenth-century warehouse, Nordatlantens Brygge promotes artistic and cultural links between Denmark, Greenland, Iceland and the Faroe Islands. A small store at the back sells a good selection of regional music and crafts such as Icelandic knitwear and sealskin slippers from Greenland.

Cafés and restaurants

CAFÉ OVEN VANDE

Overgaden Oven Vandet 44 ☎ 32 95 96 02, ⓦ cafeovenvande.dk. Daily 10am–midnight. MAP P.79, POCKET MAP F13

With tables and chairs spilling out onto the pavement, this Christianshavn institution is a fine place to enjoy an excellent lunchtime smørrebrød platter (98kr) by the canal. Catching the sunset, it's also hugely popular in the evening when a French-inspired menu takes over.

CHRISTIANSHAVNS BÅDUDLEJNING

Overgaden Neden Vandet 29 ☎ 32 96 53 53, ⓦ baadudlejningen.dk. Daily: April to mid-May 10am–6pm; mid-May to mid-Sept 9am–midnight; end Nov to Dec 11am–10pm. MAP P.79, POCKET MAP F14

Formerly a boat rental point, this partially covered floating pontoon, moored at the Torvegade bridge, is now a trendy lunch spot, serving a few select smørrebrød options (from 95kr), a range of tasty and colourful seafood salads, plus cold-cut meat platters. Open for dinner, too.

DAC CAFÉ

Strandgade 27B ☎ 32 57 19 30, ⓦ dac.dk. Mon–Fri 11am–4pm, Wed 11am–8pm, Sat & Sun 10am–4pm. MAP P.79, POCKET MAP F12

Apart from its wonderful panoramic views DAC's first-floor café is especially popular for the elaborate all-day weekend brunch (175kr), which includes home-made gravlax and waffles.

CHRISTIANIA CYKLER

KADEAU

KADEAU

Wildersgade 10A ☎ 33 25 22 23, ⓦ kadeau
.dk. Tues–Sat 6pm–midnight. MAP P.79,
POCKET MAP E14

Inspired by the Baltic island of
Bornholm, this new Michelin-
starred arrival is set in
Christianshavn a few blocks
from *Noma*. The menu features
dishes such as oysters,
octopus, beetroot and pork
belly. It ain't cheap, though,
with an eight-course,
wine-paired menu going for a
cool 1800kr. Heaven for
die-hard foodies.

KAFFESYNDIKATET

Prinsessegade 50. Mon–Fri 7.30am–5.30pm,
Sat & Sun 10am–6pm. MAP P.79, POCKET MAP F14

This cosy basement café across
from Vor Frue Kirke is
undisputedly Christianshavn's
best place for coffee (freshly
roasted and ground, of course)
and tea. Delicious home-made
cake, too.

LAGKAGEHUSET

Torvegade 45 ☎ 32 57 36 07, ⓦ lagkagehuset
.dk. Mon–Thurs & Sat & Sun 6am–7pm, Fri
6am–7.30pm. MAP P.79, POCKET MAP F14

The original *Lagkagehuset*
(there are now branches across
the city), "Layercake House"
(see p.78) is an exceptional
bakery-cum-patisserie serving
beautiful pastries (from 25kr).

MORGENSTEDET

Fabriksområdet 134, Christiania
ⓦ morgenstedet.dk. Tues–Sun noon–9pm.
MAP P.79, POCKET MAP H8

Small, welcoming vegetarian
place set in a cute little cottage
that once belonged to the army,
with tables outside in a
peaceful garden. Inexpensive
organic food includes a hot
meal of the day, such as bean
stew or potato gratin (75kr),
and a selection of salads (30kr).

NOMA

Strandgade 93 ☎ 32 96 32 97, ⓦ noma.dk.
Tues–Sat noom–10pm. MAP P.79, POCKET MAP G7

Consistently voted the world's
best restaurant, *Noma* is
peerless for otherworldly
Nordic cuisine, immaculately
presented – a menu of twenty
courses (2500kr, including
wine) in all, created by chef
René Redzepi. Ingredients are
mainly locally sourced, many of
them foraged. You'll need to
book at least six months in
advance to secure a reservation.

NOSE WISE

Vestmannagade 4 ☎ 32 96 02 20. Mon–Thurs
8am–6.30pm, Fri 8am–10pm, Sat & Sun
10am–6.30pm MAP P.79, POCKET MAP F8

Laid-back, sleek basement café
in Islands Brygge, offering
(among other things)
well-prepared breakfasts in

various combinations and delicious sandwiches, all chalked up on a large blackboard.

SPICEY KITCHEN CAFÉ

Torvegade 56 ☎ 32 95 28 29. Mon–Sat 5pm–1am, Sun 2–11pm. MAP P.79, POCKET MAP F14

Chaotic, always busy Middle Eastern café dishing up delicious and excellent-value South Asian and Middle Eastern meals – mainly curries and kebabs, with at least one vegetarian option. Prices start at 70kr for a main course.

SPISELOPPEN

Prinsessegade 1, Christiania ☎ 32 57 95 58. ⓦ spiseloppen.dk. Tues–Sat 5–10pm, Sun 5–9pm. MAP P.79, POCKET MAP G8

Considering the ramshackle staircase leading up to it, the high quality of the cuisine offered by this rustic Christiania collective comes as quite a surprise. The global reach of the menu reflects the wide origins of its chefs.

VIVA

Langebrogade Kaj 570 ☎ 27 25 05 05. ⓦ restaurantviva.dk. Daily 5.30pm–midnight (last sitting 9.30pm). MAP P.79, POCKET MAP D14

This small and intimate boat restaurant, moored next to Langebro bridge, serves up an exquisite gourmet three-course menu (350kr), plus wine menu (300kr). Don't miss a preprandial cocktail or digestif on the rooftop deck for a magical view of the city lights reflecting in the water.

Bars

HALVANDET

Refshalevej 325 ☎ 70 27 02 96. ⓦ halvandet .dk. April–Sept 10am till late. MAP P.79, POCKET MAP H4

Located on a disused industrial pier on Holmen, this unusual beach bar is decked out with mattresses (rented for sun-lounging during the daytime), while things get livelier in the evening. Nibbles and light meals are available in the daytime. Best reached via harbour bus or canal boat.

NEMOLAND

Christiania ☎ 32 95 89 31. ⓦ nemoland.dk. Mon–Thurs 10am–1am, Fri & Sat 10am–3am, Sun 10am–1am. MAP P.79, POCKET MAP G8

This lively café-bar with a large outdoor space is a popular place for visitors to sample purchases from Pusherstreet undisturbed. There are free gigs on a rickety stage outside on summer Sundays, featuring well-known Danish artists and lesser-known international acts.

Venues

ISLANDS BRYGGES KULTURHUS

Islands Brygge 18 ☎ 82 33 47 80. ⓦ kulturogfritid.kk.dk/kulturhuset-islands -brygge. Mon–Wed 10am–11pm, Thurs–Sat 10am–midnight, Sun 10am–10pm. MAP P.79, POCKET MAP E9

The waterfront Islands Brygges Kulturhus puts on a packed programme of gigs, activities (Latin dance on Tuesdays, for example) and film nights. There's also a café-bar-restaurant with a large water-facing terrace out front.

LOPPEN

Christiania ☎ 32 57 84 22. ⓦ loppen.dk. Most Wed–Sun from 9pm. MAP P.79, POCKET MAP G8

On the first floor of the warehouse that also houses *Spiseloppen* and the Infocaféen this usually tightly packed venue hosts superb live gigs five nights a week. Music ranges from Danish folk to hardcore punk, with admission 50–200kr.

Vesterbro and Frederiksberg

The two neighbouring districts of Vesterbro and Frederiksberg couldn't be more contrasting. Vesterbro was until recently a solidly working-class area. Urban regeneration projects over the past fifteen years have smartened it up, inflating the value of property, and attracting more affluent residents. They have also brought with them a slew of edgy art galleries, restaurants and bars such as those in the über-trendy, newly converted Kødbyen meat-packing area. Conservative Frederiksberg combines elegant tree-lined avenues, beautiful parks and grand villas – a stroll down Frederiksberg Allé to the romantic seventeenth-century Frederiksberg Have (gardens) and palace gives a flavour of its well-heeled opulence. The quaint little street of Værnedamsvej links the two districts with some superb places to eat and drink, exclusive shops and a neighbourly, outgoing feel.

VESTERBROGADE AND ISTEDGADE

MAP OPPOSITE, POCKET MAP E8 –B8

As one of the main arteries leading into the city, **Vesterbrogade** has been lined with restaurants and inns since the sixteenth century. Today, it offers access to the hugely popular nightlife of Kødbyen, and retains a bohemian atmosphere thanks to the large number of artists and musicians who still live here. Running roughly parallel, **Istedgade** is all that is left of the city's once infamous red-light district which flourished after the legalization of pornography in the 1960s. Today a handful of hookers and the occasional porn shop near Central Station is all that remains.

VÆRNEDAMSVEJ

Vesterbro and Frederiksberg

CAFÉS AND RESTAURANTS

Bento	15
Café Viggo	3
Cofoco	14
Elefanten	24
Famo	10
Fiskebaren	21
Frk. Barners Kælder	12
Granola	4
Hansens Gamle Familiehave	5
Lê Lê Nhà Hàng	8
Madklubben	7
Mother	17
Paté Paté	16
Riccos Kaffebar	23
Spuntino	6
Sticks N Sushi	25
Tea Restaurant	9

BARS

Bang & Jensen	18
Falernum	2
Karriere Bar	22
MARkbar	11
Mesteren & Lærlingen	19
Mikkeller	13
Pegasus	20
Salon 39	1

SHOPS

Designer Zoo	4
Donn Ya Doll	5
Meyers Deli	1
Samsøe og Samsøe	2
SummerBird	3

ACCOMMODATION

Absalon	6	Løven	6
Ansgar	10	Missionshotellet Nebo	3
Hotel Central & Cafe	1	Saga Hotel	5
Copenhagen Island	12	Sct Thomas	7
Guldsmeden Axel	4	Wake Up Copenhagen	11
Guldsmeden Bertrams	9	Zleep Hotel Centrum	8

VENUE

Vega	1

KØBENHAVNS MUSEUM

Vesterbrogade 59 ☎ 33 21 07 72,
ⓦ copenhagen.dk. Daily 10am–5pm. 40kr, Fri
free. MAP P.87, POCKET MAP D8

Easy to spot with a miniature model of medieval Copenhagen out front, the **Københavns Museum** (Museum of Copenhagen) traces the city's history using models, paintings, photos and domestic items. On the second floor a small room is devoted to author, philosopher and existentialist **Søren Kierke gaard** (1813–1855), including manuscripts of his famous works and paintings of his girlfriend, Regine Olsen. However, it's the imaginative and unconventional **temporary exhibitions**, that make the museum stand out (check the website for the latest, including the **WALL** interactive touch screen currently on tour throughout the city (see box, p.34). They also offer quirky **audio tours** of Vesterbro (free with entry ticket), by local artists and authors.

TYCHO BRAHE PLANETARIUM

Gammel Kongevej 10 ☎ 33 12 12 24,
ⓦ planetariet.dk. Mon 11.30am–7.30pm, Tues
& Sun 9.30am–7.30pm, Wed & Sat
9.30am–8.30pm, Fri 10.30am–8.30pm. Adults/
children under 12 139kr/94kr including IMAX
film, 84kr/64kr without. MAP P.87, POCKET MAP D8

Housed in a massive and unmissable yellow-brick cylinder at the foot of Sankt Jørgens lake, the city's **planetarium** is named after sixteenth-century Danish astronomer Tycho Brahe. For many visitors – especially the local schoolkids who overrun the place during the week – the main attraction is the enormous 3D IMAX screen in the planetarium's central Space Theatre, which shows science and nature films.

TYCHO BRAHE PLANETARIUM

KØDBYEN

MAP P.87, POCKET MAP D9

Once Copenhagen's former meat-packing district, **Kødbyen** is now one of the trendiest areas in the city. It encompasses cutting-edge galleries and arty cocktail bars, rustic-chic restaurants and grungy nightclubs, with a vibe that changes through the day. Until noon the feel is cold industrial, with life emanating only from the few remaining food-processing plants. After lunch, the galleries begin to open and a colourful, trendsetting crowd moves in. Come evening the restaurants pack out with diners and then partygoers who continue the evening milling from bar to bar, and later on into the nightclubs.

Kødbyen's earliest buildings – the eastern, "brown" part of the site – date back to the late nineteenth century when the city's slaughterhouses were focused on one site in a bid to improve hygiene. The original indoor cattle market is now converted into the **Øksne hallen** exhibition centre (check out the vast vaulted ceiling). In the 1930s the district was extended with the so-called "white" section to the west, whose Functionalist blue-and-white tile-covered buildings are now protected as an industrial monument.

CARLSBERG VISITOR CENTRE

Gamle Carlsbergvej 11 ☎ 33 27 12 82, ⓦ visitcarlsberg.dk. Daily 10am–5pm. 70kr.
MAP P.87, POCKET MAP B9

Carlsberg's slick visitor centre takes you through the history of the brewery and provides an insight into the interlinked history of Danes and beer. Highlights include the world's largest collection of beer bottles (over 20,000) and a wonderful assortment of old advertising campaigns. Although it lacks the noise and excitement of a large working brewery, you do get the opportunity to sample (alongside regular Carlsberg) some interesting beers from the on-site microbrewery, the **Jacobsen Brewhouse**, at the end of your visit.

The Carlsberg quarter

Exciting developments are afoot on the site of the old Carlsberg Brewery, which moved its production to a new, modern complex in Jutland in 2006. After lengthy public consultation it was decided to develop the site into a vibrant new cultural and residential quarter, **Carlsberg Byen**. The project is still in its early stages, but a number of galleries and cultural institutions have already moved in, such as **Dansehallerne** (ⓦ dansehallerne.dk), a modern-dance performance venue at Tap E, the brewery's former bottling hall, and **Galleri Nicolai Wallner** (ⓦ nicolaiwallner.com), the city's largest private gallery for contemporary art, in the old garages. You could easily spend a half-day exploring the complex. Landmark sights include the iconic **Elephant Gate**, the glorious winding Lotus Chimney, the Lime Tower lighthouse and the Star Gate, the original main entrance to the brewery. Many of Carlsberg's luscious green spaces have also been opened up to the public, including J.C. Jacobsen's tranquil garden next to the *Elefanten* café (p.92).

FREDRIKSBERG HAVE AND SLOT

Roskildevej ⓦ ses.dk. Gardens: 6am–sunset; free. Palace: guided tours Jan–June & Aug–Nov last Sat of the month 11am & 1pm; 50kr. MAP P.87, POCKET MAP A8

One of the city's most beautiful and romantic spots, **Frederiksberg Have** was originally laid out in the late seventeenth century as gardens for the recently completed royal palace. The gardens' Baroque formality was remodelled in the English landscape style a century later, with winding paths weaving across undulating lawns, boating canals and numerous follies hidden among the trees. The park can be accessed from all sides, but arriving from the *slot* gives you the best overview of its layout. Hugely popular for picnicking and lounging, the gardens also host music and theatre performances in summer (check the website for details).

Frederiksberg Slot itself, built in Baroque style, was the royal family's main summer residence until the mid-1800s, and now houses the Danish Officers Academy – it's therefore off-limits except for the infrequent guided tours.

The interior is awash with intricate stuccowork and bold and colourful ceiling paintings; grandest of all is the elaborately decorated chapel, which you may find a little over the top.

ZOOLOGISK HAVE

Roskildevej 32 ⓣ 72 20 02 00, ⓦ zoo.dk. Open from 10am; closing times vary (check website). 150kr, children under 12 90kr. MAP P.87, POCKET MAP A8

Founded in 1859, Copenhagen's **zoological gardens** encompass everything you'd expect from a zoo with over 2500 caged animals from around the globe. Aside from the wooden 44m observation tower (1905), two recently added structures stand out: Foster & Partners' etched-glass-domed **Elephant House**, complete with underfloor heating, and Danish architects Dall & Lindhardsen's **Hippo House**, where you can watch the animals frolic underwater. Both are easily visible from neighbouring parks (Frederiksberg Have for the elephants and Sønder-marken for the hippos), so – should you wish – you can avoid forking out the entrance fee to view them.

FREDERIKSBERG HAVE

Shops

DESIGNER ZOO

Vesterbrogade 137 ☎ 33 24 94 93, ⓦ zoo.dk.
Mon–Thurs 10am–5.30pm, Fri 10am–
7pm, Sat 10am–3pm. MAP P.87, POCKET MAP B8

Welcoming store run by eight
designers selling own-made
furniture, jewellery, knitwear,
pottery and glass. A great place
for that elusive Christmas gift.

DONN YA DOLL

Istedgade 55 ☎ 33 22 66 35, ⓦ donnyadoll
.dk. Mon–Fri 11am–6pm, Sat 10am–3pm.
MAP P.87, POCKET MAP D8

This chaotic clothes shop sells
sustainably produced clothes,
from bamboo underwear to
soya shirts including items
made by top Danish designers
such as Stig P and Eco Nord.

MEYERS DELI

Gammel Kongevej 107 ☎ 33 25 45 95
ⓦ eyersdeli.dk. Daily 8am–10pm.
MAP P.87, POCKET MAP C7

The original branch of what is
now a chain, selling delicious
home-made bread as well
delicacies like honey-cured
ham, home-made patés, pickles
and chutneys, and freshly
pressed apple juice.

SAMSØE OG SAMSØE

Værnedamsvej 12 ☎ 35 28 51 02, ⓦ samsoe
.com. Mon–Thurs 10am–6pm, Fri 10am–7pm,
Sat 10am–4pm. MAP P.87, POCKET MAP C8

Cool own-brand designer wear
for men and women, plus a few
items from other labels. They're
known for their simple, loose-
fitting style and punchy colours.

SUMMERBIRD

Værnedamsvej 9 ☎ 33 25 25 50,
ⓦ summerbird.dk. Mon–Fri 11am–6pm, Sat
10am–3pm. MAP P.87, POCKET MAP C8

Dinky little chocolatier selling
arguably the world's best
chocolate. Try the otherworldly

MEYER'S DELI

flødeboller (cream buns) –
fluffy, chocolate-coated
marshmallow treats.

Cafés and restaurants

BENTO

Helgolandsgade 16 ☎ 88 71 46 46, ⓦ ki.dk.
Tues–Sat 11am–2pm, 5–10pm. MAP P.87,
POCKET MAP D8

Family-run Japanese eatery
with a traditional minimalist
interior. Famous for its
makunouchi (bento) boxes –
from 298kr – it also excels in
less pricey sushi and maki rolls,
and has a well-stocked Japanese
cocktail bar. Take-out available.

CAFÉ VIGGO

Værnedamsvej 15 ☎ 33 31 18 21,
ⓦ cafeviggo.com. Mon–Wed 10am–midnight,
Thurs 10am–1am, Fri 10am–2am, Sat
11am–2am. MAP P.87, POCKET MAP C8

Named after Belgian comic-
book character Gaston (Vakse
Viggo in Danish), this
French-style café-bistro is
packed both day and night.
Apart from good, solid bistro
dishes such as quiche forestière
or steak haché, the chef excels
in genuine Breton *galettes*.

COFOCO

Abel Cathrines Gade 7 ☎ 33 13 60 60,
🖥 cofoco.dk. Daily 5.30pm–midnight.
MAP P.87, POCKET MAP D8

Bright and modern, *Cofoco*
sources much of its food from
the Baltic island of Bornholm
– where the growing season is
longer and produce conse-
quently tastier. Dishes are
superb but small (all 85kr),
the idea being that you sample
a range.

ELEFANTEN

Pasteursvej 20 ☎ 88 81 08 11,
🖥 afe-elefanten.dk. Mon–Wed 10am–9pm,
Thurs–Sat 10am–10pm, Sun 10am–5pm.
MAP P.87, POCKET MAP B9

Housed in Tap E along with
Dansehallerne (see box, p.89),
Elefanten is an essential pit stop
in the up-and-coming
Carlsberg district. Lunch
includes smørrebrød (60kr)
and sandwiches (75kr), while
the short evening menu hinges
on hearty meat dishes and
lighter pastas or risottos. Sit
either in the industrial pillared
hall or outside facing J.C.
Jakobsen's garden.

FAMO

Saxogade 3 ☎ 33 23 22 50, 🖥 famo.dk. Daily
6pm–midnight. MAP P.87, POCKET MAP C8

Small, cheerful, no-frills Italian
restaurant serving a four-
course menu (370kr), prepared
by a pair of Michelin-starred
chefs who have decided to go it
alone. Flavour-packed
delicacies might include
panzanella (Florentine
bread-and-tomato salad,
crammed with anchovies and
herbs) and *ribolita* (Tuscan
bean soup).

FISKEBAREN

Flæsketorvet 100 ☎ 32 15 56 56,
🖥 fiskebaren.dk. Mon–Thurs 5.30pm–midnight,
Fri until 2am, Sat noon–4pm & 5.30pm–2am,
Sun noon–4pm & 5.30pm–11pm .
MAP P.87, POCKET MAP D9

This super-trendy fish restaurant
in hip Kødbyen offers
sustainably sourced fresh fish
and seafood, from oysters (from
95kr for three) to Greenland
snowcrab (165kr), the menu
varying according to season and
catch. With whitewashed walls
and shiny black floors, it's also a
monument to industrial chic.

FRK. BARNERS KÆLDER

Helgolandsgade 8 ☎ 33 33 05 33,
🖥 frkbarners.dk. Daily noon–4pm &
5.30–11pm. MAP P.87, POCKET MAP D8

With outdoor seating on a
street-side terrace and a cosy
cavern-like atmosphere inside,
this traditional restaurant –
complete with red-and-white-
check tablecloths – serves
time-honoured Danish classics
such as herring platters (98kr)
at lunch, and hakkebøf (Danish
burger) with potatoes,
cucumber salad and fried egg
(149kr) at dinnertime.

GRANOLA

Værnedamsvej 5 ☎ 40 82 41 20. Mon–Fri
7am–6pm, Sat 9am–5pm, Sun 9am–4pm.
MAP P.87, POCKET MAP C8

Retro-style milkshake bar
whose decor – including
genuine 1930s ceiling lamps
from the Rover factory – shows
staggering attention to detail.
Breakfast (platters 65kr),
smoothies and juices are served
from early morning, while later
on the menu centres on
well-prepared home-made
dishes such as quiches, salads,
sandwiches – and delicious
milkshakes, of course.

HANSENS GAMLE FAMILIEHAVE

Pile Alle 10 ☎ 36 30 92 57, 🖥 hansenshave
.dk. May–Sept 11am–midnight, rest of the
year Sun until 6pm. MAP P.87, POCKET MAP B8

In a pretty garden (with a
retractable winter roof) around

the corner from Frederiksberg Slot this popular place excels in smørrebrød (herring 59kr). There's also a good range of traditional hot dishes such as fried eel with parsley sauce (239kr), and roast pork with pickled red cabbage.

LÊ LÊ NHÀ HANG

Vesterbrogade 40 ☎ 33 31 31 25, Ⓦ ele.dk. Mon–Thurs 5–10pm, Fri & Sat 5pm–10.30pm. MAP P.87, POCKET MAP D8

This spacious Vietnamese serves gorgeous dishes which you can watch being lovingly prepared in the large open kitchen. Try for instance the Saigonese papaya salad with beef and Vietnamese mint (78kr). Takeout is available further along the street at no. 56 (daily 11am–9.30pm).

MADKLUBBEN

Vesterbrogade 62 ☎ 38 41 41 43, Ⓦ madklubben.info. Daily 5.30pm–midnight. MAP P.87, POCKET MAP C8

Simple, well-prepared dishes in a funky, slightly space-age restaurant (part of a small chain) across from Københavns Museum. The straightforward concept (choose from one to four courses, 100–250kr) is a big hit with the Vesterbro crowd. Favourite mains include fish of the day and truffle-oil risotto (both 100kr).

MOTHER

Høkerboderne 9 ☎ 22 27 58 98, Ⓦ mother.dk. Mon–Wed & Sun 11am–11pm, Thurs–Sat 11am–1am. MAP P.87, POCKET MAP D8

Organic sourdough pizza served in a long, rustic butcher's hall in industrial-hip Kødbyen. *Mother*'s chipper Italian proprietor, who also mans the door, is kept busy throughout the day as hungry diners arrive in droves. Pizzas start at 75kr for a filling Marinara, and there's a small

MOTHER

but select wine list and full-flavoured Menabrea beer on draught.

PATÉ PATÉ

Slagterboderne 1 ☎ 39 69 55 57, Ⓦ patepate.dk. Mon–Wed 9am–midnight, Thurs 9am–1am, Fri 9am–3am, Sat noon–3am. MAP P.87, POCKET MAP D8

On-trend Kødbyen wine bar-cum-restaurant housed in a former meat paté factory. Apart from a vast selection of great wines, it also offers good, solid French fare, with lighter bites at lunchtime and dinner mains including onglet steak (185kr) and duck confit (190kr).

RICCOS KAFFEBAR

Istedgade 119 Ⓦ riccos.dk. Mon–Fri 8am–11pm, Sat & Sun 9am–11pm. MAP P.87, POCKET MAP C9

Riccos coffee shops have spread throughout the city but this is where it all started, and their unfaltering passion for good organic coffee is still in evidence. Packed into a tight space with only a few tiny tables and a long communal bench along the wall, coffee aficionados cram together here every morning for their caffeine fix.

SPUNTINO

Vesterbrogade 68 ☎ 70 20 50 89,
🖰 cofoco.dk. Mon–Sat 5.30pm–midnight.
MAP P.87, POCKET MAP C8

Part of the excellent Cofoco
chain, no-frills *Spuntino* offers
Italian classics such as *arancini*,
braised lamb shank and *panna
cotta*. A three-course menu
(295kr) is the only option,
with four or five choices for
each course.

STICKS'N'SUSHI

Arni Magnussons Gade 2 ☎ 88 32 95 95,
🖰 sushi.dk. Mon–Wed & Sun 10am–midnight,
Thurs 10am–1am, Fri & Sat 10am–2am.
MAP P.87, POCKET MAP D9

Great-tasting sushi, seafood
salads and much else Japanese
besides on the top floor of the
twelve-storey *Tivoli Hotel*, with
great views of Kødbyen and
beyond.

TEA RESTAURANT

Helgolandsgade 2 ☎ 33 24 58 58. Daily
noon–11pm. MAP P.87, POCKET MAP D8

Plain and verging on stark, the
decor at *Tea* feels almost as
authentically Chinese as the
home-style food. Try the
scrummy Beijing duck menu
(208kr).

Bars

BANG & JENSEN

Istedgade 130 ☎ 33 25 53 18,
🖰 .bangogjensen.dk. Mon–Fri 7.30am–2am,
Sat 10am–2am, Sun 10am–midnight.
MAP P.87, POCKET MAP C8

Housed in an old nineteenth-
century chemist with high
stucco ceilings, *Bang & Jensen* is
a cosy neighbourhood café by
day and a heaving bar at night.
Saturday night features
Ingeborg's Cocktail Salon, when
you can enjoy a daiquiri or dry
martini as the eponymous DJ
spins some ambient tunes.

FALERNUM

Værnedamsvej 16 ☎ 33 22 30 89,
🖰 falernum.dk. Mon–Thurs 8am–midnight, Fri
8am–2am, Sat 10am–2am, Sun 10am–
midnight. MAP P.87, POCKET MAP C8

This snug wood-panelled wine
bar offers most of its wines by
the glass (from 60kr), with
friendly and knowledgeable
waiters on hand to share tasting
notes. There's also a wide range
of food on offer throughout the
day, such as home-made soup
and an outstanding charcuterie
platter.

FALERNUM

KARRIERE BAR

Flæsketorvet 57 ☎ 33 21 55 09, ⓦ karrierebar.com. Thurs 8pm–midnight, Fri & Sat 8pm–4am. MAP P.87, POCKET MAP D9

Super-cool Kødbyen cocktail bar and nightclub established by sibling artists Jeppe and Lærke Hein to show off works by up-and-coming artists. With amazing cartwheel lights and DJs pumping the music, the dancefloor is crowded most Fridays and Saturdays.

MÄRKBAR

Vesterbrogade 106A ☎ 33 21 23 93. Tues–Wed 5pm–2am, Thurs–Sat 4pm–5am MAP P.87, POCKET MAP C8

Dark, grungy, Berlin-inspired rock bar with a dependable crowd of regulars nodding their heads to the rhythm. A good range of beer, too.

MESTEREN & LÆRLINGEN

Flæsketorvet 86 ☎ 32 15 24 83. Wed–Sat 8pm–3am. MAP P.87, POCKET MAP D9

Small, worn corner dive in Kødbyen with a disc-juggling DJ on Friday and Saturday. Music ranges from Pink Floyd to African Soul.

MIKKELLER

Viktoriagade 8 ☎ 33 31 04 15, ⓦ mikkellerdk. Mon–Wed & Sun 2pm–midnight, Thurs–Fri 2pm–2am, Sat noon–2am. MAP P.87, POCKET MAP D8

Mikkeller is a name whispered in hushed reverential tones among the beer cognoscenti, and this intimate and refined basement bar is a worthy adjunct to the serious business of brewing. A self-declared Carlsberg-Free Zone, it offers a superb range of innovative microbrewery ales, including twenty on tap.

PEGASUS

Mysundegade 28 ☎ 33 31 80 50, ⓦ pegasus-cph.dk. Mon–Thurs 5–11pm, Fri

MIKKELLER

5pm–1am, Sat noon–1am. MAP P.87, POCKET MAP C9

Friendly and unpretentious, *Pegasus* is a cavernous bodega-type place with outdoor seating on a peaceful street. It prides itself in its wide range of beer and wine, and tasty tapas to help soak it all up.

SALON 39

Vodroffsvej 39 ☎ 39 20 80 39, ⓦ salon39.dk. Tues 4pm–11.30pm, Wed & Thurs 4pm–12.30am, Fri & Sat 4pm–2am. MAP P.87, POCKET MAP D7

Frederiksberg's first cocktail bar, this stylish, elegant place is now also popular for the meals that accompany the cocktails – such as, the juicy 39 cheeseburger (139Kr).

Venue

VEGA

Enghavevej 40 ☎ 33 25 70 11, ⓦ vega.dk. MAP P.87, POCKET MAP C9

One of the city's top live music venues, housing three stages with sublime sound featuring well-established artists and bands through the week. The attached *Ideal Bar* offers a slightly lower-key (and much smaller) venue for catching up-and-coming local bands (60–110kr) and DJs.

Nørrebro and Østerbro

Beyond the city ramparts, the two neighbouring mid-nineteenth-century districts of Nørrebro and Østerbro are sometimes difficult to tell apart. This is despite deeply contrasting histories – Nørrebro's one of deprivation and social struggle followed by more recent immigration and gentrification, and Østerbro's characterised by traditional wealth and privilege. Aside from Copenhagen's most famous cemetery they lack standout tourist sights. They do, however, have plenty to offer when it comes to going out and having a good time with the locals. Squares such as trendy Sankt Hans Torv and multicultural Blågårdsplads in Nørrebro, and laid-back Bopa plads in Østerbro, are alive and kicking day and night, as is the once grimy Jærgersborgsgade, now one of the city's most hyped streets, thanks mostly to the presence of a Michelin-starred restaurant.

ASSISTENS KIRKEGAARD

Nørrebrogade April–Sept daily 7am–10pm,
Oct–March 7am–7pm Entrances on
Nørrebrogade, Jagtvej and Kapelvej
MAP OPPOSITE, POCKET MAP C5

The tranquil leafy cemetery of **Assistens Kirkegaard** was first established in 1760 as a burial place outside the city walls for its poor and destitute. Since then, and especially in the nineteenth century during Copenhagen's Golden Age of art and culture, it became the city's most prestigious and famous burial place. Most of the graves are of the key movers and shakers in the city's past. Pick up one of the colourfully dotted maps at one of the many entrances, each colour representing a profession, and you can make your way around to find graves of luminaries such as author Hans Christian Andersen, philosopher Søren Kirkegaard, Nobel-prize-winning physicist Niels Bohr and many, many more.

While burials still occasionally take place here, Assistens Kirkegaard has more in common with a regular park with its wide tree-lined cycle paths and picnickers and sunbathers lounging about on warm days, some using the tombstones as back rests.

FÆLLEDPARKEN

MAP P.98, POCKET MAP E3-4

Fælledparken is at half a square kilometre the city's largest park used by over 11 million visitors each year. It started life as a common used to graze the city's livestock. Later it became the favoured haunt for the city's gentlefolk on their Sunday afternoon strolls. Today you'll find all walks of life here, many of them kicking a ball around one of the six demarcated football pitches. At the corner near Trianglen a tranquil scent garden has been designed for the visually impaired, while across Edel Sauntes Allé, you'll find Northern Europe's largest skatepark, opened in 2012. On sunny days the park becomes a patchwork of sunbathers' blankets and it's often difficult to find a spare patch of grass to settle on. Various events take place in Fælledparken throughout the year. Highlights include May Day and the annual carnival which both culminate here with lots of partying. In front of the park's small café there are also occasional gigs during summer, as well as weekly f ree Salsa lessons. Check ⓦcafe-pavillonen.dk for details.

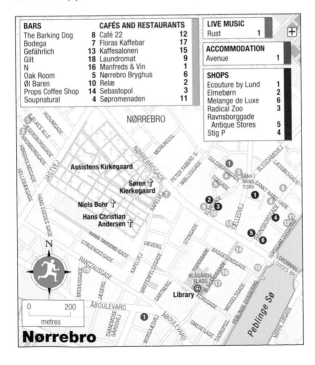

BARS		CAFÉS AND RESTAURANTS	
The Barking Dog	8	Café 22	12
Bodega	7	Floras Kaffebar	17
Gefährlich	13	Kaffesalonen	15
Gilt	18	Laundromat	9
N	16	Manfreds & Vin	1
Oak Room	5	Nørrebro Bryghus	6
Øl Baren	10	Relæ	2
Props Coffee Shop	14	Sebastopol	3
Soupnatural	4	Søpromenaden	11

LIVE MUSIC	
Rust	1

ACCOMMODATION	
Avenue	1

SHOPS	
Ecouture by Lund	1
Elmebørn	2
Melange de Luxe	6
Radical Zoo	3
Ravnsborggade Antique Stores	5
Stig P	4

Nørrebro

Østerbro

Experimentarium

0 — 200
metres

SHOPS

Enula 9	3
Langelinie	5
Normann Copenhagen	4
Paustian	1
Pour Quoi	2

CAFÉS AND RESTAURANTS

Café Sundet	1
Den Franske Café	10
Fischer	6
Fru Heiberg	8
Gourmandiet	7
Paustian	2

BARS

Bopa	4
Kafe Kapers	3
Panzon	9
Pixie	5

ACCOMMODATION

| Hotel Rye | 1 |

EXPERIMENTARIUM

Tuborg Havnevej 7 ☎ 39 27 33 33.
Ⓦ experimentarium.dk. Mon & Wed–Fri
9.30am–5pm, Tues 9.30am–9pm, Sat & Sun
11am–5pm, 165kr. MAP OPPOSITE, POCKET MAP F1

Worth a detour if you have
kids, **Experimentarium** is a
giant hands-on science lab
where you can test all things
imaginable, or so it feels. The
large permanent exhibit looks
at things such as the human
body (avoid the section on
sound waves if you don't like
loud noises), how soap bubbles
work, energy generation and
much more. A large temporary
exhibitions space often features
blockbuster attractions on loan
from other museums. Staff
(known as "pilots") are at hand
to show you what to do, if
needed. Most children are

EXPERIMENTARIUM

worn out after a day of running
around, pulling on ropes,
pushing barrels, leaving parents
free to do what they want
afterwards.

Shops

ECOUTURE BY LUND

Fælledvej 16A ☎ 27 58 57 30.
Ⓦ ecoture.dk. Fri 2–6.30pm. MAP P.97,
POCKET MAP D5

Tucked away behind a small
courtyard, this tiny shop sells
glamorous women's clothes
with a bohemain, theatrical
vibe. The "Eco" part of the
name comes from their
(oh-so Nordic) organic and
socially responsible creden-
tials. Note the extremely
limited opening hours.

ELMEBØRN

Elmegade 21 ☎ 35 35 60 65. Mon–Thurs
11am–5.30pm, Fri 11am–6pm, Sat
10am–2pm. MAP P.97, POCKET MAP D5

Gloriously cute children's
clothing, shoes, blankets and
the like – somewhat pricey but
excellent quality which lasts for
years – sold from a stylish
basement shop.

ENULA 9

Rosenvængets Allé 6 ☎ 35 38 17 85.
Ⓦ enula9.dk. Mon–Fri 11am–5.30pm, Sat
10am–2pm. MAP OPPOSITE, POCKET MAP F4

Tiny little shop selling a
beautiful selection of clothes
and accessories for pregnant
women and new-born babies.

LANGELINIE

Langelinie Promenaden Ⓦ langelinie-outlet
.dk. Daily 11am–6pm.
MAP OPPOSITE, POCKET MAP G4

A strip of designer outlet stores
– including Noa Noa and
RedGreen – located along the
pier across from where visiting
cruise ships dock.

MELANGE DE LUXE

Ravnsborggade 6 ☎ 22 63 65 75.
Ⓦ melangedeluxe.dk. Mon–Fri 11am–6.30pm,
Sat 11am–3pm MAP P.97, POCKET MAP D6

A small, packed place selling
secondhand designer wear
– such as Gucci, Prada and
Chanel – at prices that don't
require a second mortgage.

NORMANN COPENHAGEN

Østerbrogade 70 ☎ 35 55 44 59.
Ⓦ normann-copenhagen.com.
Mon–Fri 10am–6pm, Sat 10am–4pm.
MAP P.98, POCKET MAP F4

A showcase for Nordic designer
homeware, with plenty of
high-end pieces as well as a few
quirky and affordable kitchen
accessories. A fun place to see
what cutting-edge creatives can
think of next.

PAUSTIAN

Kalkbrænderiløbskaj 2 ☎ 39 16 65 65,
Ⓦ paustian.dk. Mon–Wed & Fri 9.30am–6pm,
Thurs 9.30am–6pm, Sat 10am–3pm.
MAP P.98, POCKET MAP G2

Superb designer furniture sold
in a magnificent building
designed by Jørn Utzon of
Sydney Opera House fame. The
vast range on offer includes
own-brand furniture as well as
iconic pieces such as Alvar
Aalto sofas and Verner Panton
chairs. There's also a stylish
restaurant (see p.103).

POUR QUOI

Nordre Frihavnsgade 13 ☎ 35 26 62 54.
Mon–Fri 10am–6am, Sat 10am–2pm.
MAP P.98, POCKET MAP F4

Cool clothes for women sold in
a compact three-storey shop

with heaps of fabulous dangly,
glittering accessories. Perfect
for those lusting after
leopard-print leggings or a
unique t-shirt.

RADICAL ZOO

Elmegade 19 ☎ 32 14 12 08, Ⓦ radical-zoo
.dk. Mon–Thurs 11am–6pm, Fri &
Sat 11am–5pm. MAP P.97, POCKET MAP D5

Small basement store selling
achingly on-trend clothes for
men and women from
lesser known Danish and
international designers, plus
some own-brand creations.

RAVNSBORGGADE ANTIQUE STORES

MAP P.97, POCKET MAP D6

The Nørrebrogade end of
Ravnsborggade is famous for
its antique stores. Perusing
these has become a popular
Saturday morning treat and the
prices have skyrocketed as a
consequence. You may still be
able to find some bargains if
you dig around long enough.

STIG P

Ravnsborggade 18 ☎ 35 35 75 00, Ⓦ stigp.
dk. Mon–Fri 11am–6pm, Sat 10am–4pm.
MAP P.97, POCKET MAP D5

A minimalist, slimline shop
selling quality ladieswear – own
brand as well as well-known
international names such as
Stella McCartney and Calvin
Klein.

Cafés and restaurants

CAFE 22

Sortedams Dosseringen 21 ☎ 35 37 38 27,
Ⓦ cafe22.dk. Mon–Wed & Sun
9am–midnight, Thurs–Sat 9am–2am.
MAP P.97, POCKET MAP D5

Tucked away on a quiet corner,
Café 22 is a cosy basement

PAUSTIAN

FRU HEIBERG

cafe/restaurant with a string of popular lakeside tables with blankets available when the air gets chilly. Busy all day, from breakfast onwards; the good-value menu includes a mouthwatering veggie or meaty brunch (98kr).

CAFÉ SUNDET

Svaneknoppen 2, Svanemøllen ☎ 39 29 30 35, Ⓦ cafesundet.dk. May–Sept Daily 11am–10pm, Oct–Dec & Feb–Apr Mon–Fri & Sun 11am–5pm. MAP P.98, POCKET MAP F1

On the first floor of the Svanemøllen sailing clubhouse with wonderful views of Øresund, *Café Sundet* is the perfect place for a leisurely lunch. The focus is naturally on seafood – such as baked lobster in garlic and basil (132kr) – but you also won't go wrong either with their salads or "light" pizzas (from 50kr).

DEN FRANSKE CAFÉ

Sortedams Dosseringen 101 ☎ 35 42 48 45, Ⓦ denfranskecafe.dk. Mon–Fri 9am–11pm, Sat & Sun 10am–11pm. MAP P.98, POCKET MAP F4

At the posh Østerbro end of the lakes, this delightful café with outdoor seating on the lakeside promenade features French-style décor and a few gallic touches on the menu – freshly baked croissants for example. You'll also find classic Danish rye-bread sandwiches plus some very tasty burgers (around 120kr) served with home-made *frites*.

FISCHER

Victor Borges Plads 12 ☎ 35 42 39 64, Ⓦ hosfischer.dk. Mon–Fri noon–midnight, Sat & Sun 10.30am–midnight. MAP P.98, POCKET MAP F4

Compact and romantic little Italian trattoria in the heart of Østerbro, just off Nordre Frihavnsgade, offering flavour-packed Roman dishes – such as *guancia di maiale con fagioli* (pork cheeks stuffed with cowberries) – a result of the chef's many years of training in Rome. Mains around 185kr.

FLORAS KAFFEBAR

Blågårdsgade 27 ☎ 35 39 00 18, Ⓦ floraskaffebar.dk. Mon–Thurs 10am–10pm, Fri & Sat 10am–11pm, Sun 10am–9pm. MAP P.97, POCKET MAP D6

Warm and welcoming, *Flora's* is inspired by traditional American coffee shops. The menu features savoury pancakes and home-made chilli (89kr) as well as an excellent cake selection. Don't miss the scrumptious Valrhona hot chocolate.

FRU HEIBERG

Rosenvænget Allé 3 ☎ 35 38 91 00 Ⓦ fruheiberg.dk. Tues–Sun 11.30am–4pm & 5–11pm. MAP P.98, POCKET MAP F4

Arty sleek restaurant dedicated to nineteenth-century actress, author and poet Johanne Louise Heiberg – her portraits adorn the walls. The food is beautifully prepared and mostly French influenced, including a satisfying entrecôte steak (195kr) and a much raved about cheese board.

GOURMANDIET

Rosenvænget Allé 7A ☎ 39 27 10 00,
ⓦ gourmandiet.dk. Mon–Thurs 11am–6pm,
Fri 11am–7pm, Sat 10am–3pm. By Night:
Thurs–Sat 5.30pm–midnight. MAP P.98,
POCKET MAP F4

Gourmandiet is a traditional
butcher's shop – evident in the
beautiful old tiling – which has
evolved into an excellent
charcuterie-cum-restaurant.
Although open for meaty
brunch on Saturdays, and with
a lunchtime menu comprising
an extensive selection of
delicious cold cuts during the
week, it's the juicy organic steak
three nights a week that's the
star attraction.

KAFFESALONEN

Peblinge Dosseringen 6 ☎ 35 35 12 19,
ⓦ kaffesalonen.com. Mon–Fri
8am–midnight, Sat & Sun 10am–midnight.
MAP P.97, POCKET MAP D6

An old lakeside favourite which
started life as a breakfast/coffee
shop for workers on their way
home from the nightshift and
now offers delicious meals
throughout the day, including
grilled goat's cheese salad and
ribeye steak served with all the
trimmings. Weather permitting,
service extends to a lakeside
pontoon with a lively bar –
especially worth dropping by
on Midsummer's Eve.

LAUNDROMAT

Elmegade 15 ☎ 35 35 26 72,
ⓦ thelaundromatcafe.com. Mon–Fri
8am–midnight, Sat & Sun 10am–midnight
MAP P.97, POCKET MAP D5

Hugely successful Icelandic
concept café which combines
laundromat, library and café in
one, around the corner from
trendy Sankt Hans Torv. Their
weekend brunch (138kr) comes
recommended, having won
several awards, but the place is
busy all day with students
sipping coffee and people
making use of the free wi-fi.

MANFREDS & VIN

Jægersborggade 40 ☎ 36 96 65 93,
ⓦ manfreds.dk. Tues–Fri noon–3.30pm &
5.30–10pm, Sat & Sun 10am–3.30pm &
5.30–10pm. MAP P.97, POCKET MAP C5

New Nordic fine dining in an
informal, intimate setting.
Food is adventurous featuring
ingredients such as duck
gizzard and unripe peaches,
prepared to perfection in a
sharing menu (250kr per
person). There's also a
good-value weekend brunch
(95kr) and a unique wine list
featuring "biodynamic" wines.

NØRREBRO BRYGHUS

Ryesgade 3 ☎ 35 30 05 30,
ⓦ noerrebrobryghus.dk. Mon–Thurs 11am–
midnight, Fri & Sat 11am–2am. MAP P.97,
POCKET MAP D5

Microbrewery-cum-restaurant
where you can try beer-glazed
cauliflower and *panna cotta*
served with beer syrup.
Surprisingly, it all seems to
work, and the long wood-
beamed tables are packed to
capacity most nights.
Hour-long brewery tours led by
the chief brewer (150kr)
include four samples en route.

LAUNDROMAT

PAUSTIAN

Kalkbrænderiløbskaj 2 ☎ 39 18 55 01,
ⓦ restaurantpaustian.dk. Tues–Fri
noon–4pm & 6–11pm, Sat noon–4pm
MAP P.98, POCKET MAP G2

Buzzy restaurant attached to
the top-of-the-range designer
furniture store (see p.100).
The lunchtime menu of
herring, smørrebrød and
salads (from 65kr) provides a
delicious break from furniture
perusing.

RELÆ

Jægersborggade 41 ☎ 36 96 66 09,
ⓦ restaurant-relae.dk. Wed–Sat 5.30pm–
midnight, also Sat noon–3pm.
MAP P.97, POCKET MAP C5

Probably the only Michelin-
starred restaurant in the city
that won't break the bank
(four-course tasting menu
385kr). Expect unusual Nordic
fusion food such as carrots,
elderflower and sesame. The
emphasis is on the dining
experience and you may end
up squeezed a little tight in
this unpretentious basement
restaurant. Reserve a table
well in advance – there are
also a few counter settings
facing the kitchen available at
short notice.

SEBASTOPOL

Sankt Hans Torv 32 ☎ 35 36 30 02,
ⓦ sebastopol.dk. Mon–Thurs 8am–midnight,
Fri 8am–1am, Sat 9am–1am, Sun 9am–10pm
MAP P.97, POCKET MAP D5

A Copenhagen fixture since
1994, *Sebastopol* offers a touch
of Parisian café chic on trendy
Sankt Hans Torv. It's often
packed with arty Nørrebro
types indulging in a leisurely
brunch (from 80kr). Later in
the day the French bistro menu
includes dishes such as calf
ragoût or *moules frites* (150kr).
With south-facing seating
outside on the square,
Sebastopol is also a popular
place for a sundowner drink.

SØPROMENADEN

Sortedam Dosseringen 103 ☎ 35 42 66 06,
ⓦ søpromenaden.dk. Daily 11am–11pm
MAP P.97, POCKET MAP D5

With chequered tablecloths and
a lovely lakeside setting,
Søpromenaden emanates rural
charm even though it's at the
lake's busy and chic Østerbro
end. Menu highlights include
an extensive lunchtime
smørrebrød list and all-time
Danish classics such as
frikadeller and *rødkål* –
meatballs served with pickled
red cabbage (75kr).

Bars

THE BARKING DOG

Sankt Hans Gade 19 ☎ 35 36 16 00.
Ⓦ thebarkingdog.dk. Mon–Thurs 4pm–1am.
Fri & Sat 4pm–2am, Sun 4pm–midnight.
MAP P.97, POCKET MAP D5

When you've had enough of the city's über stylish offerings this relaxed neighbourhood pub may come in handy. Featuring a small selection of beers (including a few from Nørrebros Bryghus) and wine, *The Barking Dog* also makes a mean Power's Sour cocktail; ask the waiter for the story.

BODEGA

Kapelvej 1 ☎ 35 39 07 07, Ⓦ bodega.dk.
Mon–Thurs 10am–midnight, Fri & Sat
10am–3am, Sun 10am–9pm. MAP P.97.
POCKET MAP D5

Charming neighbourhood bar-restaurant facing the yellow-brick walls of the Assistens Cemetery. Sup on some wonderful craft beers (many from Nørrebros Bryghus), good food and awesome hot chocolate during the day. Things get lively on Friday and Saturday evenings when the DJ hits the decks.

BOPA

Løgstørgade 8 ☎ 35 43 05 66, Ⓦ cafebopa
.dk. Mon–Wed 9am–midnight, Thurs
9am–2am, Fri 9am–5am, Sat 10am–5am, Sun
10am–midnight. MAP P.98, POCKET MAP F3

Cosy café-bar which gets packed most weekends after 11.30pm when a DJ hits the turntables. Excellent range of beers including some from the Skovlyst Brewery north of the city which uses quirky ingredients such as nettles and beech syrup for flavouring.

GEFÄHRLICH

Fælledvej 7 ☎ 35 24 13 24, Ⓦ gefahrlich
.dk. Tues & Wed 5pm–midnight, Thurs

5pm–3am, Fri & Sat 5pm–4am. MAP P.97.
POCKET MAP D5

Berlinesque café, restaurant, cocktail bar and nightclub in one (oh, and a hairdressers, too). Once service finishes at the restaurant, the cocktail waiters take over, and the DJ cranks up some floor fillers (club slogan: "fuck you if you can't dance").

GILT

Rantzausgade 39 ☎ 27 26 80 70.
Ⓦ gilt.dk. Wed–Sat 6pm–2am.
MAP P.97, POCKET MAP C6

"Honest and unadulterated classic cocktails" goes the sales pitch at this stylish little bar. While you might persuade them to knock up a martini, the ephasis here is on Nordic-inspired concoctions using unusual ingredients such as dandelion syrup and roasted pine needles.

KAFE KAPERS

Gunnar Nu Hansens Plads 2 ☎ 35 25 11 20.
Ⓦ kafekapers.dk. Mon–Wed & Sun 9am–
midnight, Thurs–Sat 9am–2am.
MAP P.98, POCKET MAP E3

On a square a short walk from Fælledparken (p.97), *Kapers* is basically a glass cube encased in a large marquee. The outdoor seating area is a popular place to watch the world go by thoughout the year (heaters and blankets provided in winter).

N

Blågårdsgade 17 ☎ 32 15 68 52.
Ⓦ cafe-n-2200.dk. Mon–Sat 8am–10pm, Sun
9am–9pm. MAP P.97, POCKET MAP D6

A chilled-out little place with long tables and benches on lively Blågårdsgade and the perfect spot to absorb the day's last rays of sunshine. Drinks on offer include organic beer and wine, and some wonderful freshly made juices.

ØL BAREN

OAK ROOM

Birkegade 10 ☎ 38 60 38 60, ⓦ oakroom.dk.
Wed 7pm–1am, Thurs 7pm–2am, Fri 4pm
–4am, Sat 6pm–4am. MAP P.97, POCKET MAP D5

Super cool, Mad-Men-esque
cocktail bar whose sleek
interior, designed by cutting-
edge architect Kasper Røøn,
transports you back to those
heady 1960s days of Danish
Functionalism. Don't miss the
Venezuelan Butterfly (made
with passion fruit, mint and
rum), the all-time classic.

ØL BAREN

Elmegade 2 ☎ 35 35 45 34, ⓦ oelbaren
.dk. Mon 9pm–1am, Tues–Thurs 4pm–1am, Fri
3pm–1am, Sat 1pm–1am, Sun 1–11pm.
MAP P.97, POCKET MAP D5

A small, bar run for and by
beer nerds – and proud of it.
Don't expect conversation to
drift far from the favoured
subject – brews from around
the globe – and you'll be fine.
Featuring over one hundred
different labels, there's plenty to
talk about.

PANZON

Rosenvængets Allé 6 ☎ 35 38 98 00,
ⓦ panzon.dk. Tues–Thurs 5pm–midnight,
Fri 4pm–2am, Sat 5pm–1am.
MAP P.98, POCKET MAP F4

Romantic little wine bar in the
posh end of Østerbro with a
vast range on wines on offer
(starting at 60kr for a glass)
plus a good selection of tapas
to soak up the plonk.

PIXIE

Løgstørgade 2 ☎ 39 30 03 05, ⓦ cafepixie
.dk. Mon–Thurs 8am–1am, Fri 8am–3am,
Sat 10am–3am, Sun 10am–1am.
MAP P.98, POCKET MAP F3

Facing a small playground on
Bopa Plads, *Pixie* is an
authentic neighbourhood café
(breakfasts from 50kr), popular
with parents relaxing on the
outdoor terrace. Occasional live
music in the evenings.

PROPS COFFEE SHOP

Blågårdsgade 5 ☎ 35 36 99 55,
ⓦ propscoffeeshop.dk. MAP P.97, POCKET MAP D6

Quirky bar-cum-café with a
slightly chaotic, laid-back
atmosphere. All of its rickety
furniture is for sale – look out
for the price tag underneath.

SOUPANATURAL

Guldbergsgade 7A ☎ 32 13 17 35,
ⓦ soupanatural.dk. Mon–Wed & Sun
11.30am–10pm, Thurs 11.30am–midnight, Fri
& Sat 11.30am–2am MAP P.97, POCKET MAP D5

Tiny place specialising solely in
organic soups and cocktails
("Don't panic, it's Organic!").
Fortunately the odd combina-
tion works because business is
booming, not least with
punters warming up for gigs at
Rust (below) across the street.

Live Music

RUST

Guldbergsgade 8 ☎ 35 24 52 00, ⓦ rust.dk.
Wed–Sat 9pm–5am MAP P.97, POCKET MAP D5

Three floors of live music with
edgy, experimental as well as
more mainstream acts and a
kickass clubbing scene too
(40–60kr). Named after Cold
War aviator Mathias Rust.

Day-trips

An afternoon away from the big city is essential for getting to know a gentler, quieter Denmark. Copenhagen is just a short train ride or even cycle from some stellar destinations in greater Zealand. If you're staying in town for more than just a day or two, you'll definitely want to venture north on a train (and take your rented cycle with you if you like) for art museums, parklands and castles galore – including the very fortress that inspired Shakespeare's Elsinore Castle in *Hamlet*. South, meanwhile, you'll find beaches, quiet townships, more art and Scandinavia's biggest and best aquarium.

DYREHAVEN AND BAKKEN

Klampenborg S-Tog station. Bakken ☎ 39 63 35 44, ⓦ bakken.dk. March–Aug Mon–Thurs 9am–5pm & Fri 9am–4.30pm; Sept–Feb Mon–Thurs 8.30am–3.30pm, Fri 8.30am–3pm. Admission free; multi-ride pass 249k, children 179kr. MAP OPPOSITE.

A short walk from Klampenborg S-Tog station, the largely forested **Dyrehaven** (Deer Park) was established in 1669 as a royal hunting ground, and is still home to some two thousand (fairly tame) red, sika and fallow deer. It's a picturesque spot, with the ancient oak and beech woodland an atmospheric backdrop, particularly in the early morning mist. Poised on a hilltop in the middle of the park is the **Eremitageslotten** (Ermitage Palace), a grand hunting lodge built for Christian VI in 1736, though it's closed to the public.

Occupying part of the park's southern section, **Bakken** is supposedly the world's oldest still-functioning amusement park, tracing its origins back to 1583 when entertainers first set up business next to Kirsten Piil's holy spring. It lacks Tivoli's polish or refinement – but with 33 rides and almost as many places to drink, there's plenty of fun to be had, not least at weekends when it can be heaving.

DYREHAVEN

Day-trips

LOUISIANA

Humlebæk train station, from which it's a 10min walk (follow the signs). ☎ 49 19 07 19, ⓦ louisiana.dk. Tues–Fri 11am–10pm, Sat & Sun 11am–6pm. 95kr. MAP P.107.

A perfect fusion of art, architecture and landscape, **Louisiana Museum of Modern Art** – with good reason Denmark's most visited art gallery – has a setting nearly as magical as the museum itself. Overlooking the Øresund strait, the museum began life in 1958, when a series of interconnecting glass pavilions was built around a nineteenth-century villa, Louisiana (named after the original owner's three wives, each of whom, oddly enough, was called Louise) – the ensemble landscaped within an outdoor sculpture park. Louisiana's collection grew quickly and the museum is now home to over three thousand permanent works from around the globe, many world-class.

The entrance is in the main villa, from which – moving clockwise into the west wing – you first reach a light, open space primarily used for temporary shows; exhibitions in recent years have included Andy Warhol, David Hockney, Ai Weiwei and Paul Klee. Next, housed in a purpose-built gallery, is an outstanding collection of **Giacometti**'s gaunt sculptures and drawings, which leads on to the museum's extensive and colourful collection of abstract works by **CoBrA** (see p.71). Major Danish artists such as Henrik Heerup and Asger Jorn – who has a special room dedicated to his art – are featured alongside.

From the museum café, with its outdoor terrace overlooking Øresund, a subterranean section of graphic art leads onto another of the museum's highlights, the permanent exhibition in the museum's south wing, which focuses on **Constructivism** with works by the likes of Vasarely, Albers and Soto. **Nouveau Réalisme** is represented with pieces by Yves Klein, César and Raysse among others, while Lichtenstein, Rauschenberg, Warhol and Oldenburg lead the charge for the **Pop Art** and **Minimalism** collections.

Outside, on the lawns sloping down towards the coast, the **sculpture garden** is home to around sixty works including Max Ernst, Henri Laurens, Miró and Henry Moore.

LOUISIANA

FREDERIKSBORG SLOT

S-train line E to Hillerød, then bus 301 to Ullerød or 302 to Sophienlund ☎ 48 26 04 39, ⓦ dnm.dk. Daily April–Oct 10am–5pm, Nov–March 11am–3pm. 75kr. MAP P.107.

Glorious **Frederiksborg Slot** lies decorously across three small islands within an artificial lake, and is set within magnificent Baroque gardens. It was originally the home of Frederik II and birthplace of his son Christian IV, who, at the beginning of the seventeenth century, had it rebuilt in an unorthodox Dutch Renaissance style. It's the unusual aspects of the design – a prolific use of towers and spires, Gothic arches and flowery window ornamentation – that still stand out.

Since 1882, the interior has functioned as a **Museum of National History** with sixty-odd rooms charting Danish history since 1500. Many are surprisingly free of furniture and household objects, drawing attention instead to the ranks of portraits along the walls – a motley crew of flat-faced kings and thin consorts who between them ruled and misruled Denmark for centuries.

KRONBORG SLOT

Helsingør train station, from which it's a 15min walk. ☎ 49 21 30 78, ⓦ kronborg.dk. Easter–May & Sept & Oct daily 11am–4pm, June–Aug daily 10am–5.30pm, Nov–Easter Tues–Sun 11am–4pm. 75kr. Guided tours of the royal chambers in English daily at 11.30am and 1.30pm; of the casemates daily 11am & 1pm. MAP P.107.

Tactically placed on a sandy curl of land extending seawards into the Øresund some 45km north of Copenhagen in the city of Helsingør, **Kronborg Slot** is impossible to miss. It's known primarily – under the name of Elsinore Castle – as the setting for Shakespeare's

FREDERIKSBORG SLOT

Hamlet, though it's uncertain whether the playwright actually ever visited Helsingør.

Constructed in the fifteenth century by Erik of Pomerania, the original fortress of Krogen was for hundreds of years the key to control of the Øresund (Helsingborg on the other side of the strait was also under Danish rule), enabling the Danish monarchs to extract a toll from every ship that passed through it.

MARITIME MUSEUM OF DENMARK

Kronborg Slot ☎ 49 21 06 85, ⓦ www.fs.dk. Jan–Easter & Nov–Dec Tues–Sun 11am–4pm, Easter–May & Sept–Oct daily 11am–4pm, June–Aug daily 10am–5.30pm. MAP P.107.

Denmark's newest museum is set underground in the old dry docks next to Kronborg Castle. Built at a cost of 13 million kroner and opened in mid-2013, the structure comprises a continuous ramp looping around the dock walls, allowing for unobstructed views of the castle. Inside, informative and interactive exhibits span Viking, medieval and modern seafaring, exploration and merchant shipping (including a colossal Maersk freight container).

BLUE PLANET

AMAGER STRANDPARK

Metro to Øresund Station or Bus #77 or 78
☎ 33 66 33 19, ⓦ www.amager-strand.dk.
MAP P.107.

Just to the southeast of the centre of Copenhagen, beyond Christianshavn, is the large island of **Amager**. On its east coast, with fine views of the Øresunds Bridge, **Amager Strandpark** is one of the city's most popular summer getaways, with around 5km of beautiful, soft sandy beaches. The beautifully restored traditional wooden **Helgoland Søbadean-stalt**, where Øresundsvej meets Amager Strandvej, offers free changing facilities and showers (June–Aug; free), while at the southern end, **Kastrup Søbad** (June & Aug Mon–Fri 3–6pm, Sat & Sun 11am–6pm, July 11am–8pm; free) has a 5m-high trampoline which provides a fabulous launch pad into the water.

Connected to "mainland" Amager by three short bridges is an artificial island some 2km long, with a shallow lagoon, popular for kite surfing, windsurfing and kayaking and ideal for kids to paddle in. There are toilets and showers all along the beach, and at its southern end a couple of good places to eat (see p.112).

BLUE PLANET (DEN BLÅ PLANET)

Metro to Kastrup Station, from which it's a 10min walk ☎ 44 22 22 44, ⓦ www .denblaaplanet.dk. Mon 10am–9pm, Tues–Sun 10am–6pm. 160kr, children 85kr. MAP P.107.

In a spectacular waterside position next to Kastrup marina, **Den Blå Planet** (The Blue Planet) was opened in 2013 to provide a state-of-the-art new home for Denmark's National Aquarium. All curves, it's a remarkable structure, shaped – when viewed from the air – like a giant whirlpool, with five "arms" radiating from the vortex centre, a circular foyer. Each arm represents a different environment: habitats range from a sunken Amazon forest, featuring Europe's largest school of piranhas, to a Faroese bird cliff, complete with puffins and divers. Highlight for many, though, is undoubtedly the walk through the huge "ocean" aquarium tunnel, with hammerhead sharks and manta rays swimming above and below you and inquisitive sea lions pressing up to the glass. The building has already won several design awards, and is among the best spots in the city to cut loose (and curry favour with) the kids for an afternoon.

ARKEN MUSEUM OF MODERN ART

Train to Ishøj station, then bus #128 (10min), or a 20min walk ☎ 43 54 02 22. ⓦ www.arken.dk. Tues & Thurs–Sun 10am–5pm, Wed 10am–9pm. 95kr. MAP P.107.

Smaller and more manageable than Louisiana or the Statens Museum for Kunst, the **Arken Museum for Moderne Kunst** (Arken Museum of Modern Art), just outside the coastal town of Ishøj about 20km southwest of Copenhagen, is well worth seeking out both for its architecture and for its content. Paying homage to its bleak position in front of a windswept sandy beach, architect Søren Robert Lund designed the museum to resemble a shipwreck, its prow thrusting dramatically up from among the dunes. The museum is known for its excellent temporary exhibitions – recent shows have covered CoBrA artist Carl-Henning Pedersen and Frida Kahlo – though these merely supplement a permanent display that focuses on contemporary art from the 1990s onwards and includes pieces by Damien Hirst, Antony Gormley, Jeff Koons and Grayson Perry as well as Danish artists Per Kirkeby and Asger Jorn. An additional plus for Arken is its café, which is well worth extending your visit for (see p.112).

DRAGØR

Tårnby Station, then bus #350S to the end. Museum: ☎ 30 10 93 07, ⓦ www .museumamager.dk. May–Sept Tues–Sun noon–4pm. 30kr, children free. MAP P.107.

South of Copenhagen Airport, in the southeasternmost corner of Amager, lies the atmospheric cobblestoned fishing village of **Dragør**, formerly the departure point for ferries to Sweden. It now mainly survives on tourism and the high incomes of its city-commuting inhabitants – properties in Dragør do not come cheap. Apart from meandering around the quaint streets, and lazing on the peaceful south coast beaches, while here you could check out the **Dragør Museum**, devoted to the maritime history of the village from the thirteenth-century herring trade to the arrival of the Dutch in the early sixteenth century.

Rocking Roskilde

The carnivalesque, four-day **Roskilde festival** (ⓦ www.roskilde-festival .com) might be the single best open-air event in Europe, commonly drawing some 100,000 people. At the end of June, throngs of Danish teens, kidults and ageing hipsters descend on a Roskilde farm to make merry and hear well over 150 Scandinavian and international acts take the stage (nine stages, actually). Metallica and Rihanna were recent performers, but Roskilde is best for lesser-known, up-and-coming acts you wouldn't typically hear anywhere else. Logistically, it's all done rather well, with a free camping ground next to the festival site and regular shuttle buses from the train station. Tickets typically run in excess of 2000kr and regularly sell out, so plan and purchase in advance.

Roskilde (30min by train from Copenhagen) is also home to the wonderful **Viking Ship Museum** (daily 10am–5pm; 115kr; ⓦ vikingeskibsmuseet.dk), one of Denmark's premier attractions and home to five well-preserved Viking longships. In summer you can row a modern version in the harbour.

Cafés and restaurants

ARKEN MUSEUM CAFÉ

ALLEHÅNDE

Havkajakvej 16, Amager Strandpark
☎ 53 60 30 38, ⓦ allehaandecafe.dk.
Mon–Thurs 11am–6pm, Fri & Sat 11am–9pm.

A modern houseboat in a fine setting on Amager Strandpark, *Allehånde* ("Allspice") offers tapas (35kr per tapa) to die for – make your choice from a list of options on a blackboard – and first-rate sandwiches (grilled veg and hummus 65kr). It's manned by hearing-impaired staff (with an interpreter) and run by a social foundation that aims to guide them into permanent employment.

ARKEN MUSEUM CAFÉ

Skovvej 100, Ishøj ☎ 51 67 02 23,
ⓦ arken.dk. Tues & Thurs–Sun 10am–4.30pm,
Wed 10am–8.30pm.

Beautiful herring platters (89kr) and sandwiches served in an elegant café upstairs in the museum, with sweeping views of marram grass-covered dunes and the deep blue sea in the distance. The menu also includes a handful of tasty hot dishes – baked cod with kale, for instance – and the obligatorily excellent cake (35kr).

CAFÉ KYSTENS PERLE

Bryggergården 14, Kastrup ☎ 32 50 40 19,
ⓦ cafekystensperle.dk. Mon–Fri 11am–10pm,
Sat & Sun 10am–10pm.

A short walk from Den Blå Planet, this striking eighteenth-century restaurant was once a brewery. With its crooked walls and low ceilings the "Pearl of the Coast" has retained some of its old-fashioned ambience while its front terrace provides great coastal views. Food is served throughout the day, including brunch (fruit platter 45kr), a lunchtime smørrebrød platter (139kr) and burgers (125kr) and steak later in the day.

CAFÉ SYLTEN

Søndre Strandvej 50, Dragør ☎ 32 94 01 49,
ⓦ sylten.dk. Mon–Fri noon–11pm, Sat & Sun
11am–11pm.

Hidden away among the dunes a stone's throw from the beach just south of Dragør, this old dark-wood cabin is a wonderful place to catch the sunset on a summer evening. Come for a drink on the terrace (there's a small but select beer and wine list) or to sample some hearty meat dishes (from 99kr). At weekends there's a brunch buffet (149kr; 11am–2pm)

DRAGØR RØGERI

Gammel Havn 6-8, Dragør ☎ 32 53 06 03,
ⓦ dragor-rogeri.dk. Thurs 11am–4pm,
Fri–Sun 10am–4pm.

Authentic smokehouse at Dragør harbour that sells an enormous array of freshly caught and freshly smoked seafood, including legendary smoked eel and herring.

They're suppliers to the main restaurants in the city but you can cut out the middleman and enjoy their home-made *fiskefrikadeller og remoulade* (fishcakes with tartare sauce) or fried plaice and chips (both 50kr) at their harbourfront picnic table for half the price.

PETER LIEPS HUS

Dyrehaven 8 ☎ 39 64 07 86, ⓦ peterliep.dk. Tues–Sun 11am–9pm.

Quaint thatched restaurant on a busy pedestrian junction at the edge of Dyrehaven woods, not far from the Bakken amusement park. Lunch at *Peter Lieps* is a popular weekend treat for busy city folk, with a menu focusing primarily on smørrebrød – with an extensive list of over twenty toppings – and classics such as a delicious venison burger made with local game. Mains are in the 130–145kr range.

RESTAURANT PIIL & CO

Dyrehaven 7, Klampenborg ☎ 70 26 02 12, ⓦ piil-co.dk. Daily noon–5pm.

Tucked away in Dyrehaven next to the famous holy spring of Kirsten Piil and

overlooking a lake, this romantic log cabin is a great place for pancakes and hot chocolate after a day in the woods. For more substantial dining there is also an excellent lunchtime spread of smørrebrød classics and a few à la carte dishes such as saddle of pork with apple and crackling (125kr). Just a ten-minute walk from Klampenborg station.

SPISESTEDET LEONORA

Frederiksborg Slot, Møntportevej 2, Hillerød ☎ 48 26 75 16, ⓦ leonora.dk. Daily 10am–5pm.

Housed in one of Frederiksborg Slot's former stables, with seating outside in the palace courtyard in summertime, *Leonora* serves a traditional Danish lunch that's fit for a king. Lavishly presented smørrebrød, tartlets overflowing with asparagus and chicken, fillets of plaice served with prawns and caviar, all very reasonably priced.

Bar

SKY BAR

Bella Sky Comwell Hotel, Ørestaden. Take Metro to Bella Center or Bus 30 from Vesterport ☎ 32 47 30 00, ⓦ bellaskycomwell .dk. Mon–Thurs noon–1am, Fri & Sat noon–2am, Sun noon–11pm.

On the top floor of the extraordinary *Bella Sky* hotel – a vast, 814-room complex – the *Sky Bar* provides breathtaking views of the city skyline and across to Sweden. It's accessed via the super-cool aerial walkway that links the two twisting leaning towers. Drinks here are worth sampling, too: there's a good selection of champagnes and wines, or a gin and tonic will set you back 95kr.

PETER LIEPS HUS

Malmö

Just a short hop across the water from Copenhagen, the Swedish city of Malmö makes for a tempting day-trip. Once part of Denmark (the Danes spell it "Malmø"), it was acquired by the Swedish king Karl X in 1658 along with Skåne (Scania), the surrounding province. Today Malmö is Sweden's third largest city, an attractive mix of chocolate-box medieval squares and striking modern architecture, most notably the Turning Torso skyscraper, Scandinavia's tallest building. You'll also find it a cosmopolitan, culturally diverse population – more than a hundred languages are spoken on its streets and Turkish and Thai food are as popular as meatballs and herring.

STORTORGET AND LILLA TORG

The city's main square, **Stortorget** is as impressive today as it must have been when it was first laid out in the sixteenth century. It's flanked on one side by the imposing **Rådhus**, built in 1546 and covered with statuary and spiky accoutrements. To its rear stands the fine Gothic **St Petri Kyrka** (daily 10am–6pm; free) while to the south runs **Södergatan**, Malmö's main pedestrianized shopping street.

A late sixteenth-century spin-off from Stortorget, **Lilla Torg** is everyone's favourite part of the city. Lined with cafés and restaurants, it's usually pretty crowded at night, with drinkers kept warm under patio heaters and bars handing out free blankets.

MALMÖHUS CASTLE

Malmöhusvägen ☎ 040 34 44 00, ⓦ malmo.se. Daily 10am—5pm. 40SEK. MAP P.115.

The princely **Malmöhus** is a low fortified castle defended by a wide moat and two circular keeps. Built by Danish king Christian III in 1536, the castle was later used for a time as a prison, but it now houses the **Malmö Museer**, a disparate but fascinating collection of exhibitions on everything from geology to photography – and an aquarium, too. The pleasant

Visiting Malmö

Frequent **trains** (34min; 90kr) connect Copenhagen with Malmö, across the 16km Öresund bridge/tunnel link. You arrive in the bowels of Malmö's rebuilt Central Station. **Malmö Airport** is located 30km to the east with frequent bus connections into the city as well as to Copenhagen. The **tourist office**, opposite the train station at Skeppsbron 2 (Mon–Fri 9am–7pm, Sat & Sun 9am–4pm, reduced hours in winter ☎ 040 34 12 00, ⓦmalmotown.com), sells the Malmö City Card (100SEK) which offers a range of discounts. Many shops accept Danish Kroner though at an uncompetitive 1-1 rate so it's usually best to convert to Swedish currency (SEK).

Malmö

CAFÉS AND RESTAURANTS

Årstidarne by the Sea	1
Barista Fair Trade Coffee	7
Bastard	3
Café Siesta	6
Dolce Sicilia	2
Krua Thai	8
Rådhuskällaren	4

SHOPS

Åhléns	2
Form & Design Center	1
Uma Bazaar	3

BARS

Malmö Brygghus	9
Mello Yello	5

grounds, the **Kungsparken**, are peppered with small lakes and an old windmill.

MODERNA MUSÉET

Gasverksgatan 22 ☎ 040 68 57 937 Ⓦ modernamuseet.se. Tues–Sun 11am–6pm. 70SEK. MAP P.115.

Opened in 2009, this branch of Stockholm's famous modern art museum hosts excellent temporary exhibitions. The building itself is worth a visit for the striking orange-red cube extension built on to what was the city's electricity works.

THE TURNING TORSO

A good twenty-minute walk or five-minute cycle ride north of the station is Malmö's most iconic sight, the 190m **Turning Torso** skyscraper. A spiralling helix of glass and steel, the structure was completed in 2005 and now lords it over the

sea towards Denmark. Heading coastwards takes you to a viewpoint of the 8km **Öresund Bridge**, the longest road-and-rail bridge in Europe. There's also access to the Ribban, Malmö's artificial sandy beach.

TURNING TORSO

Shops

ÅHLÉNS CITY

Södergatan 15 ☎ 040 24 13 00,
Ⓦ ahlens.se. Mon-Fri 10am-8pm, Sat
10am-7pm, Sun 11am-6pm. MAP P.115.

Malmö's glitziest department
store, packed with Swedish
designer labels including Acne
and Nudie Jeans.

FORM & DESIGN CENTER

Lilla Torg 9 ☎ 040 664 51 50,
Ⓦ formdesigncenter.com. Tues-Sat
11am-5pm, Sun noon-4pm. MAP P.115.

This gallery-café-shop has a lot
to offer including a good
selection of Scandinavian
design knick-knacks, and some
handmade items (tea cosies,
candlestick holders and the
like) by local artists.

UMA BAZAAR

Per Wijersgatan 9 ☎ 040 12 30 85,
Ⓦ umabazaar.se. Mon-Fri 11am-6pm,
Sat 11am-5pm. MAP P.115.

Fair Trade shop sells everything
from Indian pillows and
African carpets to recycled
jeans and wooden watches.
Being Swedish it's all resolutely
stylish, organic and sustainable.

BASTARD

Cafés and restaurants

ÅRSTIDERNE BY THE SEA

Dockgatan 1 ☎ 040 23 34 88,
Ⓦ arstidernabythesea.se. Mon-Fri
11.30-11pm, Sat 5-11pm. MAP P.115.

Large glass-fronted seafood
restaurant located at the marina
in the Western harbour area.
The menu centres on primarily
locally and sustainably sourced
produce such as lovely
pan-fried cod (175SEK) and a
wonderful seafood soup.

BARISTA FAIR TRADE COFFEE

Södra Förstadsgatan 24 ☎ 040 97 26 06,
Ⓦ baristafairtrade.com. Mon-Fri 7am-9.30pm,
Sat &-Sun 9am-9.30pm. MAP P.115.

This award-winning café chain,
now with branches across
Sweden, is the place to head for
coffee snobs. Perfectly poured,
ethically sourced and organic.

BASTARD

Mäster Johansgatan 11 ☎ 040 12 13 18,
Ⓦ bastardrestaurant.se. Tues-Thurs 5pm-
midnight, Fri & Sat 5pm-2am. MAP P.115.

Yes, you read that right. This
hip gastropub-style restaurant,
run by tatooed young chef
Andreas Dahlberg, has brought
nose-to-tail dining to Malmö,
be it pig cheek, heart trotters or
tongue. Don't miss the
Bastarrdplanka, a mix of
sausages, hams and pâte served
on a wooden board. Excellent
wines too. Mains from 195SEK.

CAFÉ SIESTA

Hjorttackegatan 1 ☎ 040 611 10 27,
Ⓦ siesta.nu. Mon 4pm-11pm, Tues-Thurs
3-11pm, Fri 3pm-12.30am, Sat
11.30am-12.30am, Sun 11.30am-8pm. MAP P.115.

Terrific little café, popular for
brunch on weekends when you
can enjoy the likes of smoked

ÅRSTIDERNE BY THE SEA

salmon smørrebrod (75SEK) and french toast. Evening mains include *moules frites* with organic mussels (176SEK).

DOLCE SICILIA

Drottningtorget 6 ☎ 040 611 31 10, ⓦ dolcesicilia.se. Mon noon–8pm, Tues–Sun 11am–6pm. MAP P.115.

A proper Italian-run *gelateria* with delicious organic ice cream made fresh every day, as well as coffee and ciabatta. Also a prime people-watching spot.

KRUA THAI

Möllevångstorget 12 ☎ 040 12 22 87, ⓦ kruathai.se. Mon 11am–3pm, Tues–Fri 11am–10pm, Sat 1–10pm, Sun 2–10pm. MAP P.115.

Affordable, authentic Thai food just south of the centre on Möllevångstorget. Pad Thai 89SEK. Unlicensed.

RÅDHUSKÄLLAREN

Stortorget ☎ 040 79 020, ⓦ profilrestauranger.se/radhuskallaren. Mon–Wed 11.30am–2pm & 5–10.30pm, Thur–Sat 11.30am–2pm & 5–11pm. MAP P.115.

Historic restaurant in the vaulted cellar of the town hall, serving a good-value lunch buffet (100SEK including salad, cheese and coffee) and a sophisticated à la carte dinner menu featuring meaty mains such as pork tenderlion or cajun fried chicken (from 169SEK).

Bars

MALMÖ BRYGGHUS

Bergsgatan 33 ☎ 040 20 96 85 ⓦ malmobrygghus.se. Mon–Tues 5pm–1am, Wed–Sat 4pm–1am. MAP P.115.

Sup pale ales, pilsners and porters at the city's only microbrewery, a ten-minute walk south of the old centre. The attached pub is open late and on Fridays and Saturdays you can take a tour of the brewery itself (195SEK).

MELLO YELLO

Lilla Torg 1 ☎ 040 30 45 25, ⓦ melloyello.se. Mon–Fri 3.30pm–1am, Sat & Sun noon–1am. MAP P.115.

This stylish bar is the best of the bunch on Lilla Torg. The long list of cocktails is supplemented by some good draught beers including Brooklyn lager. Food ranges from delicious tapas (139SEK for five dishes) to excellent seafood: try the Västerbot-tenpie, a Swedish speciality featuring cheese and fish roe.

ACCOMMODATION

Hotels

Hotels do not come cheap in Copenhagen, hovering around the 800kr–1200kr (£90–130/€110–160) mark for an average double room in high season (late June to early September). Those close to sights of Tivoli and the Inner City (Indre By) are particularly expensive, while the Vesterbro area is the city's budget hotel district with Helgolandsgade in particular lined with more affordable options. Facilities offered at most places are ultra-modern, boasting fabulous design and eco-concious features in true Danish style. The prices listed below are based on two adults sharing the cheapest en-suite double room in high season 2013 inclusive of tax (25 percent). If breakfast costs extra we have indicated in the review. Online discounts and opting for a shared bathroom can reduce prices significantly.

Tivoli and Rådhuspladsen

CAB-INN CITY > Mitchellsgade 14 ☎ 33 46 16 16, ⓦ cabinn.com. MAP P.33, POCKET MAP B14 Newish budget hotel around the corner from Central Station and a stone's throw from Tivoli, *Cab-Inn*'s main forte – apart from its compact and super functional ferry-cabin style rooms – is its central yet relatively quiet location away from the hubbub of Vesterbro. Rooms sleep up to three people. Part of a larger chain with hotels in Frederiksberg (Vordroffsvej 55 and Danasvej 22) and a new place in Ørestaden (Arne Jakobsens Allé 2) designed by Daniel Libeskind. Breakfast 70kr. **675kr**

HOTEL NIMB > Bernstorffsgade 5 ☎ 80 10 00 00, ⓦ hotel.nimb.dk. MAP P.33, POCKET MAP A13 Fairytale hotel located upstairs in Tivoli's Moorish inspired Nimb building from 1909. With just fourteen individually decorated extravagant rooms this is Copenhagen's original boutique hotel. Features include open fireplaces, antique wooden furniture and sweeping views of the gardens. *Hotel Nimb*'s opulence encompasses in-room massage (for 1050kr an hour) and a private chauffeur service (1000kr to be picked up at the airport). **2800kr**

PALACE HOTEL > Rådhuspladsen 57 ☎ 33 14 40 50, ⓦ palacehotelcopenhagen.com. MAP P.33, POCKET MAP B12 Wonderful Art Nouveau hotel from 1910 located next door to the Rådhus. A recent refurbishment has reinstated its original decor, featuring lovely details such as George Jensen silver door handles and abstract artwork on the walls. During its heyday many a Hollywood star stayed here including the likes of Audrey Hepburn and Gregory Peck. Although restored to their original appearance, rooms have been totally modernised with comfy beds and luxurious bathrooms. Breakfast 165kr. **1590kr**

RADISSON BLU ROYAL HOTEL > Hammerichsgade 1 ☎ 33 42 60 00, ⓦ radissonblu.com/royalhotel -copenhagen. MAP P.33, POCKET MAP A13 The *Royal Hotel* is an Arne Jakobsen masterpiece and a prominent example of Danish Modernist architecture. A twenty-two storey rectangular grey and green structure, the hotel is today graced with his furniture throughout, including the famous Swan, Egg, and Drop chairs which were designed specifically for the hotel. Although modern luxury abounds, the hotel today also has a funky time-warped feeling, not least as you step into the 1960s lobby. For the full retro experience book the Arne Jacobsen suite (Room 6060) which comes in at an eye-watering 5500kr a night. Breakfast 100kr. **1425kr**

THE SQUARE > Rådhuspladsen 14 🕿 33 38 12 00, Ⓦ thesquarecopenhagen.com. MAP P.33, POCKET MAP A12 Stylish, smart hotel conveniently located for easy access to Tivoli and the downtown shopping district. Housed in a former office block, the tastefully decorated minimalist rooms – spread over five floors – come with all of the required mod-cons discreetly tucked away. The breakfast restaurant on the sixth floor offers some great views of the city. Breakfast 178kr. **From 1625kr**

HOTEL TWENTYSEVEN > Løngangstræde 27 🕿 70 27 56 27, Ⓦ hotel27.dk. MAP P.33, POCKET MAP B13 Good-value designer hotel slap bang in the city centre and a minute's walk from the Rådhus (whose bells toll every fifteen minutes until midnight and from 7am in the morning, so worth bearing in mind if you're a light sleeper). With spacious modern rooms and a popular courtyard where cocktails from the hotel's *Honey Ryder* cocktail bar can be devoured. Breakfast 70kr. **1175kr**

Strøget and the Inner City

D'ANGLETERRE > Kongens Nytorv 34 🕿 33 12 00 95, Ⓦ www.dangleterre .com. MAP P.40–41, POCKET MAP E11 Recently reopened after being refurbished from top to bottom, this prestigious hotel dating from 1755 is Copenhagen's answer to *The Ritz* in London; hotel of choice for anyone who's anyone, from rock stars to US presidents. Offering classic elegance, with modern Danish design kept to a minimum (although you will find Bang & Olufsen TV screens above the bath tubs), the hotel encompasses a five-hundred square-metre luxurious spa and fitness centre, a grand restaurant, and a new champagne bar with over 160 different

champagnes on the menu. Breakfast 250kr. **5500kr**

HOTEL SANKT PETRI > Krystalgade 22 🕿 33 45 91 00, Ⓦ sktpetrihotel .com. MAP P.40–41, POCKET. MAP B11 Ultra-stylish design hotel housed in a former five-storey functionalistic department store. The spacious rooms have dark parquet flooring and sleek Scandinavian furniture such as the super-comfortable Jensen bed. Full of business travellers during the week; you can usually pick up competitive deals at weekends. Breakfast 145kr. **1435kr**

Nyhavn and Frederiksstad

71 NYHAVN > Nyhavn 71 🕿 33 43 62 00, Ⓦ 71nyhavnhotel.com. MAP P.59, POCKET MAP F11 Two inter-connected converted warehouses overlooking Inderhavnen and next door to the city's new playhouse, *71 Nyhavn* is a charming place to stay. Although slightly on the small side, the magnificent location easily makes up for this shortfall. Superior rooms feature pretty French doors opening onto a balcony. Primarily a business hotel, there are some good deals to be had during summer. Breakfast buffet 170kr. **1190kr**

ADMIRAL HOTEL > Toldbodgade 24 🕿 33 74 14 14, Ⓦ admiralhotel.dk. MAP P.59, POCKET MAP F11 Romantic waterfront hotel in a vast converted warehouse from 1787 with lots of its original features still intact such as vaulted brick ceilings and enormous wooden beams. There are 300 rooms spread over six floors, each with its own unique charm; a sea view will cost extra. Breakfast is served in the downstairs restaurant *Salt* (p.67) which is also a good bet for other meals, or simply to hang out in its waterfront café section. Breakfast 140kr. **1825kr**

HOTEL ESPLANADEN > Bredgade 78 ☎ 33 48 10 00, ⓦ firsthotels.com /our-hotels/hotels-in-denmark /copenhagen/first-hotel-esplanaden. MAP P.59, POCKET MAP G6 Excellent-value perfectly adequate hotel in this otherwise expensive regal neighbourhood of Frederikstaden, overlooking peaceful Churchill Parken and the grassy ramparts of Kastellet. The carpeted and somewhat dull rooms are a tad on the small side but so is the price, so – hey – you can't really complain. Breakfast buffet 70kr. **795kr**

SØMANDSHJEMMET BETHEL > Nyhavn 22 ☎ 33 13 03 70, ⓦ hotel-bethel.dk. MAP P.59, POCKET MAP F11 A former hostel for Icelandic sailors, *Bethel*'s superb location overlooking Nyhavn Kanal and the bars and restaurants on the opposite bank can hardly be bettered. Bearing this in mind, the somewhat dated but perfectly comfortable, clean and tidy rooms are excellent value. Ask at reception for a tour or the sailor's church round the back if that's what floats your boat. **945kr**

Rosenborg and around

IBSEN > Vendersgade 23 ☎ 33 13 19 13, ⓦ ibsenshotel.dk. MAP PP.70–71, POCKET MAP A10 Arty hotel situated on a Nansensgade street corner with bright and airy rooms spread over five floors in two interconnected nineteenth-century apartment buildings. Works by local artists (some for sale) are on display throughout the hotel, and the management even accept art for part payment of rooms (see ⓦ artmoney.org). Discounted access to Ni'Mat spa next door for 125kr. Breakfast 130kr. **1600kr**

JØRGENSEN > Rømersgade 11 ☎ 33 13 81 86, ⓦ hoteljoergensen .dk. MAP PP.70–71, POCKET MAP A10 Superb value, slightly rundown

hotel-cum-hostel a stone's throw from Torvehallerne. housing a range of rooms in different shapes and sizes, a few with en-suite bathrooms. The tightly packed dorms sleep six to ten and there is no internet access. Breakfast buffet 35kr (included if you book a private room). **Dorm beds 160kr, Doubles 750kr**

Christianshavn and around

CPH LIVING > Langebrogade 1C ☎ 61 60 85 46, ⓦ cphliving.com. MAP P.79, POCKET MAP D14 Absolutely gorgeous hotel boat with twelve identical smartly furnished rooms all facing Christian IV's redbrick brew house on the opposite bank. Reception is unstaffed and you need an access code to get in, which is given to you when you pay for the room. The reception area doubles as a help yourself breakfast buffet, which you can eat on the sundeck while taking in the fine views and fresh sea air. Moored next to it is the restaurant boat *Viva* (see p.85). **1460kr**

Vesterbro and Frederiksberg

ABSALON > Helgolandsgade 15 ☎ 33 24 22 11, ⓦ absalon-hotel .dk. MAP P.87, POCKET MAP D8 Large good-value family-run hotel offering a wide range of accommodation from small basic rooms sharing a bathroom in the corridor to en-suite doubles and triples. None of the rooms are particularly plush but the friendly and relaxed atmosphere at the hotel, and a glorious breakfast buffet included in the price to boot, makes it a good home away from home. Internet access is free in the lobby but charged extra in the rooms. **1025kr**

ANSGAR > Colbjørnsensgade 29 ☎ 33 21 21 96, ⓦ ansgarhotel.dk. MAP P.87, POCKET MAP A14 Small, friendly recently renovated family hotel in what used to be the dodgy red light district of Vesterbro. The no-frills tidy rooms are superb value and the price

Our top places to stay

For a damn-the-cost weekend: *D'Angleterre* p.121

For romance: *Hotel Central & Café* below

For luxury on a budget: *Hotel Twenty Seven* p.121, *Guldsmeden Bertrams* below

For peace and quiet: *Copenhagen Island* below

For Danish design: *Radisson Blu Royal Hotel* p.120

Location, location: *CPH Living* opposite

Watching the pennies: *Løven* below, *Copenhagen Downtown* p.125

includes a lavish breakfast buffet which in summer is served on an outdoor terrace. **900kr**

HOTEL CENTRAL & CAFE >

Tullinsgade 1 ☎ 40 82 41 20 Ⓦ centralhotelogcafe.dk. MAP P.87, POCKET. MAP C8 Set above an appropriately tiny (five-seat) coffeeshop and once inhabited by a cobbler, this one-room spot definitely earns its billing as "the smallest hotel in the world". A bed, bathroom and flat-screen TV are squeezed into the twelve-metre-square room that nevertheless beckons with some real attention to detail and olde-worlde charm. **1500kr**

COPENHAGEN ISLAND >

Kalvebod Brygge 53 ☎ 33 38 96 00, Ⓦ copenhagenisland.dk. MAP P.87, POCKET MAP D9 New on the city's hotel map, *Copenhagen Island* is as sleek as it gets. With wonderful large windows looking out to the Copencabana harbour pool just outside, you could be excused to think that you're on a seaside holiday. Inside the stylish rooms are beautifully furnished with modern Danish design and top of the range electronics. In the hotel basement there's a fitness centre with steam bath and sauna. Breakfast 150kr. **1195kr**

GULDSMEDEN AXEL >

Helgolandsgade 8 ☎ 33 31 32 66, Ⓦ hotelguldsmeden.dk/axel. MAP P.87, POCKET MAP D8 Among the city's most appealing boutique hotels with beautiful Balinese-inspired decor and superb attention to detail. This is where the supermodels come to stay and you're likely to feel like one of them after a couple of days, your every whim being catered for by the super attentive

staff. Given the level of pampering, all this comes at a very reasonable price. Breakfast buffet 165kr. **1490kr**

GULDSMEDEN BERTRAMS >

Vesterbrogade 107 ☎ 33 25 04 05, Ⓦ hotelguldsmeden.dk/bertrams. MAP P.87, POCKET MAP C8 Another of the Guldsmeden (Dragonfly) boutique hotel chain (see above), this one styling French colonial decor with wonderful dark wooden furniture and the occasional fake fur laying around. Not as large as the *Axel* branch, *Bertrams* has a slightly more personable and intimate feel, not least as the intimidating fashion-week types don't tend to stay here. Breakfast 140kr. **1490kr**

LØVEN > Vesterbrogade 30 ☎ 33 79

67 20, Ⓦ loevenhotel.dk. MAP P.87, POCKET MAP D8 A basic hotel on noisy Vesterbrogade, the real benefit of *Løven* is its excellent value and the lively and very helpful owner who runs it as a tight ship. The plain rooms come with up to five beds, some sharing facilities, others en suite. Though there's no breakfast on offer, there's a fully fitted kitchen should you wish to self-cater. Wi-fi is only available in the kitchen. **529kr**

MISSIONSHOTELLET NEBO >

Istedgade 6 ☎ 33 21 12 17, Ⓦ nebo .dk. MAP P.87, POCKET MAP D8 Age-old Danish Mission hotel whose profits all go to a Vesterbro homeless shelter behind Central Station. Rooms are nothing to write home about but perfectly pleasant and clean, some with en-suite bathroom, others sharing shower and toilet in the corridor. Breakfast buffet 50kr. **550kr**

SAGA HOTEL > Colbjørnsensgade

18-20 ☎ 33 24 49 44, Ⓦ sagahotel .dk. MAP P.87, POCKET MAP D8 In the once grotty red light district of Vesterbro, family-run *Saga* is today one of the city's really good budget options and popular with backpackers who've had their fill of rowdy and impersonal hostels. The sparsely decorated rooms sleeping up to five mostly share facilities although there are also a few en-suite rooms. Filling breakfasts are served on the first floor in a cosy dining area. **800kr**

SCT THOMAS > Frederiksberg Allé 7
☎ 33 21 64 64, ⓦ hotelsctthomas .dk. MAP P.87, POCKET MAP C8 Popular small Frederiksberg hotel housed in a nineteenth-century apartment block not far from lively Værnedamsvej and offering simple uncluttered rooms. The buffet breakfast, served in the newly excavated basement, is one of the best in town. Free internet only in the lobby. **795kr**

WAKE UP COPENHAGEN > Carsten Niebuhrs Gade 11 ☎ 44 80 00 00, ⓦ wakeupcopenhagen.com.
MAP P.87, POCKET MAP D9 Super efficient and slightly impersonal, this brand-new budget hotel on the edge of Vesterbro overlooks the railway line to one side and Inner Havnen to the other. Spread over nine floors, the 500-odd a/c rooms verge on the small side but feel perfectly adequate thanks to the clever design and layout created by architect Kim Utzon. Larger rooms and rooms with a better view cost more. Breakfast 60kr. **850kr**

ZLEEP HOTEL CENTRUM >
Helgolandsgade 14 ☎ 70 23 56 35, ⓦ zleephotels.com. MAP P.87, POCKET MAP D8 No-frills accommodation a stone's throw from Central Station, this

really is as Spartan as it gets. Hence the very reasonable prices, particularly if you book far in advance. Part of a wider Zleep concept chain, the hotel provides largely self-service accommodation with food and drink available from vending machines – although the basic breakfast buffet (69kr) is manned. Rooms sleep up to four. **499kr**

Nørrebro and Østerbro

AVENUE > Åboulevard 29 ☎ 35
37 31 11, ⓦ avenuehotel.dk. MAP P.97, POCKET MAP C6 Out from the centre on the border between Nørrebro and Frederiksberg, *Avenue* has three key things going for it: the spacious classically furnished rooms, free parking, and very reasonable rates. It also has the added bonus of not being part of a chain, which gives it that personable vibe that makes you feel right at home. **1000kr**

HOTEL RYE > Ryesgade 115
☎ 35 26 52 10, ⓦ hotelrye.dk. MAP P.98, POCKET MAP E4 Homely *Hotel Rye* is a brilliant option away from the city centre yet near the lively lake area of Østerbro and the tranquil Fælledparken. Housed in a former care home, the sixteen highly individualised rooms are spread over the second and third floors of an apartment building. All have shared bathroom in the hall (you are provided with a kimono and slippers for nocturnal visits). Outside the back yard is equipped with a play area for kids, and in the cosy dining area freshly baked rolls are available with breakfast every morning. **800kr.**

Hostels

Copenhagen has some excellent hostels that can often rival budget hotels in terms of value and style. Many offer private doubles, twins and triples as well as the usual dorm rooms. Be aware that the latter are often packed with rowdy Swedish students during the summer holidays and availability can be an issue at these times. Danhostel (⒲ danhostel.dk) which runs two of the hostels below charges a one-off membership fee of 70kr if you don't hold a Hostelling International card. Note that Jørgensen (see p.122) also offers dorm beds.

COPENHAGEN DOWNTOWN > Vandkunsten 5 ☎ 70 23 21 10, ⒲ copenhagendowntown.com. MAP PP.40–41, POCKET MAP C12 Though affiliated to Danhostel, *Copenhagen Downtown* has a hip, independent feel with guests sprawling on bean bags out onto the pavement, and a cool retro Scandinavian design. The location right next to some superb music venues and a plethora of watering holes is also hard to beat. Rooms are on the smallish side sleeping two to ten people in bunk beds, usually with shared bathroom, but everything is clean tidy and the vibe energetic. Breakfast 65kr. **Dorm beds 210kr, Rooms 660kr**

DANHOSTEL CITY > H. C. Andersens Boulevard 50 ☎ 33 11 86 86, ⒲ danhostelcopenhagencity.dk. MAP P.33, POCKET MAP C14 Modern five-star hostel housed in Denmark's first high-rise building, dating from 1955. Encompassing over a thousand beds in four-, six-, eight -and ten-bed rooms spread over sixteen floors it offers wonderful views over Copenhagen. Add the interior design by GUBI and facilities such as a bar/café in the lobby and games rooms in the basement and you could be forgiven for thinking that you're staying at a modern hotel albeit one with bunk beds. Breakfast 74kr. **Dorm beds 225kr, doubles 575kr**

GENERATOR > Adelgade 5-7 ☎ 78 77 54 00, ⒲ generatorhostels .com. MAP PP 70–71, POCKET MAP D10 Part of a Europe-wide chain of funky hostels, this one is housed in an apartment block designed by Phillip Starck. It's one of the best places to stay in town if you're young and adventurous, but like your creature comforts. All rooms come with en-suite bathrooms and range from twin-bed doubles to (pink) female dorms sleeping six and mixed dorms sleeping eight. The hostel also offers plenty of places to chill out including a large outdoor terrace and a spacious lounge/bar boasting an enormous TV. Breakfast 55kr. **Dorm beds 250kr, doubles 720k**

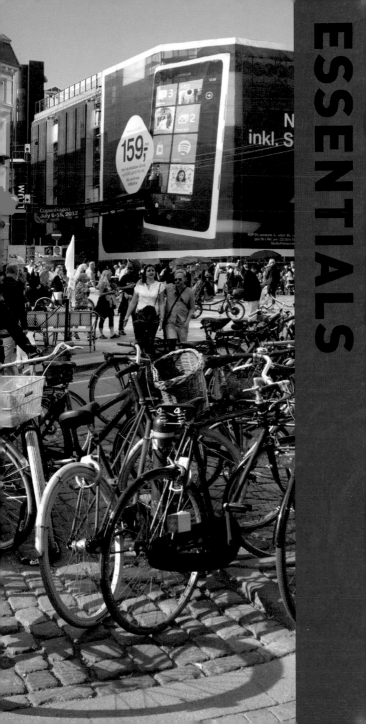

Arrival

However you arrive in Copenhagen you'll find yourself within easy reach of the city centre. Copenhagen Airport is just a few kilometres to the southeast, on the edge of the island of Amager, while almost all trains and buses deposit you near the city's main transport hub, Central Station.

By air

Getting into the city from **Copenhagen Airport** (wcph.dk), 11km from the city in the suburb of Kastrup, couldn't be easier: one of Europe's fastest airport-to-city rail lines runs directly to Central Station (roughly every 10min; 14min; 36kr). In addition, the metro (every 4–6min during the day, every 15–20min midnight–7am) links the airport with Christianshavn (12min), Kongens Nytorv (13min) and Nørreport (15min) stations (all 36kr) in the centre. Copenhagen Airport is in Zone 3 (see opposite). A taxi to the centre costs about 250kr – there's a rank outside the arrivals hall.

You can pick up free maps from the helpful information desk in sleek Terminal 3 (daily 6.10am–11pm). They also sell Copenhagen Cards (see box opposite). The airport has two late-opening banks (daily 6am–10pm), lots of ATMs, free wi-fi throughout, 72-hour luggage storage lockers (see p.132), numerous car-rental agencies and a post office. The stylish *Hilton Hotel*, connected to the airport by a pedestrian walkway, is a good place to kill some time – their lobby bar is equipped with arrival and departure screens.

Buses from small **Malmö Airport** in Sweden (wswedavia.com/malmo; see box, p.114) are integrated with flight arrivals. Some 60km east of Copenhagen it has retained its role as hub for budget flights to the city. The one-hour bus journey with Gråhundsbus (wgraahundbus.dk; 100kr) skirts around Malmö itself before crossing the magnificent Öresund Bridge (p.115), reason enough in itself to opt for the cheaper airfare option.

By bus and train

All buses and trains to Copenhagen arrive at or near **Central Station** (in Danish, Hovedbanegården or København H), the city's main transport hub, from where there are excellent connections to virtually every part of the city via bus or local train – and as from 2017 also a new metro circular line (see opposite). The station also has an array of shops, a foreign-exchange bureau (daily 8am–9pm), places to eat and, downstairs, left-luggage lockers (see p.132). The national train company, DSB, has a travel agency and information centre just inside the main entrance off Vesterbrogade (Mon–Fri 7am–8pm, Sat 8am–4pm, Sun 8am–5pm ☎70 13 14 15, wdsb.dk) and easy-to-use ticket machine in the hallway (daily 4.30am–2.40am).

Eurolines coaches from around Europe stop behind the station on Ingerslevgade, across from DGI-byen. Buses from Malmö airport stop in front of *Plaza Hotel* next to the station.

Getting around

The best way to explore Copenhagen is either to walk or cycle: the inner city is compact, much of the central area pedestrianized, and there's a comprehensive network of excellent bike paths. For travelling further afield, there's an integrated network of buses, metros, S-Tog (urban rapid transit) and local trains.

The Copenhagen Card

If you plan to do lots of sightseeing, you might want to buy a **Copenhagen Card**. Valid for 24, 42, 72 or 120 hours (299kr/449kr/529kr/749kr), it covers public transport (including Helsingør and Roskilde) and gives free (or discounted) entry to most museums. This can save a lot of money – especially since it can also give you twenty- to fifty-percent off car rental, ferry rides and theatre tickets. You can either book the card in advance online at ⊕www.copenhagencard.com or pick one up on arrival at the airport, visitor centre or Central Station.

Tickets

All city transport operates on a **zonal system** encompassing the metro, trains and buses. The city centre and immediate area, as you'd expect, are in zones 1 and 2. The cheapest ticket (**billet**) costs 24kr and is valid for one hour's travel within any two zones, with unlimited transfers between buses and trains. Another option is the **klippekort** (from 150kr), a discount card containing ten stamps, each valid for an hour's travel. Two or more people can use the same *klippekort* simultaneously, provided you clip the required number of stamps, and the 208kr version gets you as far as the airport. There's also an excellent-value **24-hour ticket** (130kr), which is valid on all transport to as far away as Helsingør and Roskilde, as well as night buses. Finally, if you're planning on visiting lots of museums and attractions, the Copenhagen Card (see box above) also includes free transport.

Tickets can be bought on board buses or at train stations, while *klippekort* and 24-hour tickets are only available at bus or train stations and HT Kortsalg kiosks. Route maps can be picked up free at stations, and most free city maps include bus lines and a diagram of the S-Tog and metro network. For more information see ⊕moviatrafik.dk/dinrejse/tourist.

The metro

Copenhagen's fast and efficient underground **metro system** (⊕m.dk) circumvents the Central Station in a "U" shape, connecting the island of Amager and Copenhagen airport with west Copenhagen via Christianshavn and Kongens Nytorv. The metro's two lines – M1 and M2 – cross the S-Tog and regional trains at Nørreport, Flintholm and Vanløse. A new circular line, due to open in 2017, will integrate more effectively with the S-Tog system stopping also at Hovedbanegården and Østerport. Metro stations are marked by a large red underlined "M" painted onto aluminium pillars.

S-Tog and regular trains

The **S-Tog** rapid transit service (⊕s-tog.dk) is laid out in a huge "U" shape and covers the whole Copenhagen metropolitan area. Six of its seven lines stop at Central Station, with the others circling the centre. Each line has a letter and is also colour-coded on route maps. Stations are marked by red hexagonal signs with a yellow "S" inside them.

Regular national trains are run by the **Danish State Railway** (DSB; ⊕dsb.dk) and among other towns connect the city to Helsingør and Roskilde, calling at Østerport and Nørreport stations and some suburban destinations on the way.

Buses

The city's **bus** network (ⓦmovi-atrafik.dk) is more comprehensive than the S-Tog system and can be a more convenient way to get around once you get the hang of finding the stops – marked by yellow placards on signposts – and as long as you avoid the rush hour (7–9am & 5–6pm). The vast majority stop at Rådhuspladsen next to Tivoli. Buses with an "S" suffix only make limited stops, offering a faster service – check they make the stop you require before you get on. Buses with an "A" suffix indicate that the bus runs frequently. All buses have a small electronic board above the driver's seat displaying both the zone you're currently in and the time – so there's no excuse for not having a valid ticket. A skeletal **night-bus** (*natdrift*) runs once or twice an hour, when fares double. Night-bus numbers always end with "N".

Harbour buses

A cheaper way to experience Copenhagen from the waterfront than a canal tour (see box opposite), yellow **harbour "buses"** sail along the harbour between Nordre Toldbod (near the Little Mermaid) and the Royal Library, stopping six times and costing the same as a normal bus fare. Services (daily every 20min about 7am–7pm) are cancelled when the harbour is frozen.

Cycling

If the weather's good, the best way to see Copenhagen is to do as the locals do and get on your bike. The superb, city-wide cycle lanes make **cycling** very safe and bikes can be taken on S-Tog trains (12kr) through any number of zones. Lights are mandatory at night (you'll be stopped and fined if the police catch you without them). Despite a recent campaign to promote wearing helmets few locals do so. You can usually **rent bikes** through your hotel or hostel (around 100kr per day). Otherwise try Københavns Cyklebørs, Gothersgade 157, Indre By (Mon–Fri 9am–5.30pm, Sat 10am–1.30pm; ☎33 14 07 17, ⓦcykelboersen.dk; 75kr per day, 350kr per week, 300kr deposit); Pedal Atleten, Oslo Plads 9, next to Østerport Station (Mon–Fri 8am–6pm, Sat 10am–3pm; ☎33 33 85 13, ⓦpedalatleten.dk; 85kr per day, 375kr per week, 500kr deposit); or Baisikeli, Turesensgade 10, Indre By and Ingerslevsgade 80 (Daily 9am–4/6pm; ☎26 70 02 29, ⓦbaisikeli.dk; from 50kr per day, 270kr per week, 200kr deposit).

Taxis

Taxis are plentiful, but with a flat starting fare of 24kr, then 140kr per kilometre (15–17.90kr after 4pm and at weekends), they're only worth taking in a group. There's a handy rank outside Central Station; you can also book with Taxa (☎35 35 35 35) or hail one in the street – the green "Fri" sign on top shows it's available. Rickshaw-styled **cycle taxis** (April–Oct; ☎35 43 01 22, ⓦrickshaw.dk), carrying a maximum of two people, operate a flat starting fare of 40kr if you flag them down on the street, then charge 4kr per minute.

Directory A-Z

Addresses

The street name is always written before the house number, which is followed by the apartment number or floor the apartment is on, followed by the side the apartment is at (t.h. – to the right as you come up the stairs, and t.v. – to the left). So,

Guided Tours

As well as the operators below, the Copenhagen Visitor Centre on Vesterbrogade (see p.133) has a long list of English-language guided walking tours many of which are free.

Bike Copenhagen with Mike ☎26 39 56 88, ⓦbikecopenhagenwithmike. dk. Cycle tours to Vesterbro, Amalienborg, the Little Mermaid, Christiania and much more, led by the knowledgable and charismatic Mike. No booking required. 290kr including bike. Cash only.

Copenhagen Sightseeing Tours ⓦsightseeing.dk. A variety of bus tours (including hop on-hop off routes which cover stretches by canal boat) with multilingual headphone commentary. From 155kr.

Copenhagen Food Tours ☎50 12 36 45 ⓦcphfoodtours.dk. Two-hour (Tues—Fri 2.30pm, 300kr) and four-hour (Tues—Sat 10am; 600kr) walking tours sampling tasters from the latest movers and shakers on the Danish food scene. The tasters along the way add up to a full-blown meal, so best to arrive hungry. Tours start and end at Torvehallerne.

Kajak Ole ☎40 50 40 06, ⓦkajakole.dk. Kayak tours (April–Oct) giving a unique view of the city from the water. Choose between a 90min paddle around Christianshavn to a 3hr circumnavigation of Slotsholmen. From 295kr including a canalside drink. Tours start from in front of *Færge Caféen*.

Netto-Bådene ☎32 54 41 02, ⓦhavnerundfart.dk. Excellent value one-hour canal tours departing from Holmens Kirke and taking in Nyhavn, Holmen, Nyholm, Amalienborg Palace and the Little Mermaid. 40kr

for instance Læssøesgade 16 3 t.h., means the third floor apartment to the right, in building number 16 on Læssøesgade. The city is divided into postal districts consisting of four digits followed by the area so Indre By is Kbh K preceded by a four-digit number; Østerbro is Kbh Ø, Nørrebro Kbh N, Vesterbro Kbh V, Amager Kbh S and Frederiksberg Fred. After the completion of the bridge across to Sweden the city of Malmö is jokingly called Kbh M.

Cinema

For the big screen experience the best option is Imperial (Ved Vesterport 4 ☎70 70 12 02, ⓦkino .dk) where international blockbusters are screened. More alternative films are shown at Grand Teatret (Mikkel Bryggersgade 8 ☎33 15 16 11, ⓦgrandteatret.dk) and Vester Vov

Vov (Absalonsgade 5 ☎33 24 42 00, ⓦvestervovvov.dk).

Crime

Despite what you may have seen on *The Killing*, Copenhagen has an extremely low crime rate. Keep an eye on your cash and passport and you should have little reason to visit the **police**. If you do, you'll find them courteous and usually able to speak English. The central police station is at Polititorvet 14 (☎33 14 88 88), with another branch at Central Station (☎33 25 14 48).

Electricity

The Danish electricity supply runs at 220–240V, 50Hz AC; sockets generally require a two-pin plug. Visitors from the UK will need an adaptor; visitors from outside the EU may need a transformer.

Emergency numbers

Dial ☎112 for police, fire or ambulance.

Embassies and consulates

Australia Dampfærgevej 26, 2nd floor ☎70 26 36 76; Canada Kristen Bernikowsgade 1 ☎33 48 32 00; Ireland Østbanegade 21 ☎35 47 32 00; South Africa Gammel Vartov 8, Hellerup ☎39 18 01 85; UK Kastelsvej 36-40 ☎35 44 52 00; US Dag Hammerskjölds Allé 24 ☎33 41 71 00.

Gay and lesbian Copenhagen

Copenhagen is one of the world's top gay destinations. Attitudes are very tolerant and there is a lively gay scene enjoyed by many straight people, too. The Copenhagen Pride festival (see p.134) is a particularly great time to experience gay Copenhagen. Check out ☺www .copenhagen-gay-life.dk for what's on.

Health

There are **24-hour emergency departments** at Bispebjerg Hospital, Bispebjerg Bakke 23 (☎35 31 23 73) and Hvidovre Hospital, Kettegårds Alle 30 ☎36 32 25 53. If you need a **doctor**, call ☎33 15 46 00 (Mon–Fri 8am–4pm). For **dental emergencies**, contact Tandlægevagten, Oslo Plads 14 ☎35 38 02 51 (Mon–Fri 8am–9.30pm, Sat & Sun 10am–noon).

The city's two main 24-hour **pharmacies** are Steno Apotek, Vesterbrogade 6C in front of Central Station (☎33 14 82 66) and Sønderbro Apotek, Amagerbrogade 158, Amager (☎32 58 01 40).

Internet

Copenhagen has plenty of wireless hubs in cafés and bars and on trains. Most hotels and hostels – and even some campsites – offer wi-fi (most for free), and access is also available **free** at libraries (though not the Royal Library).

Left luggage

The DSB Garderobe office downstairs in Central Station **stores luggage** for 55/65kr per item per day and has lockers (Mon–Sat 5.30am–1am, Sun 6am–1am; 50kr/60kr for 24hr). Copenhagen airport's left-luggage facility, in Parking House P4 across the road from terminal 2 (daily 6am–10pm), has small and large lockers for 50kr and 75kr per day respectively (max 3 days).

Lost property

The police department's **lost-property** office is at Slotsherrensvej 113, Vanløse ☎38 74 88 22. For items lost on a bus, contact the bus information office on ☎36 13 14 15 (Mon–Fri 7am–9.30pm, Sat & Sun 8am–9.30pm); for items lost on a train or S-Tog, there's a lost luggage office at Central Station (Mon–Fri 8am–8pm, Sat & Sun 10am–5pm) or contact them on ☎24 80 06 60 (Mon–Fri 10am–3pm); Copenhagen Airport also has a lost property line ☎32 47 47 25.

Money

The Danish currency is the **krone** (plural kroner), made up of 100 øre, and comes in notes of 1000kr, 500kr, 200kr, 100kr and 50kr, and coins of 20kr, 10kr, 5kr, 2kr, 1kr, 50øre and 25øre. At the time of writing, the exchange rate was approximately 8.60kr to the pound, 7.45kr to the euro and 5.70kr to the US dollar. For the latest rates, go to ☺xe.com.

PIN codes are always required when paying by card. If your card is lost or stolen, PBS Net (24hrs ☎44 89 27 50) can block your card.

Opening hours

Shops tend to open Mon—Thurs 10am—6pm, Fri 10—7pm, Sat 10am—4pm, Sun noon—4pm but shops in the centre of town tend to have longer hours. Most offices are open Mon—Fri 9am—4/4.30pm.

Phones

You should be able to use your **mobile phone** in Denmark though it may be cheaper to invest in a Danish SIM card on arrival. For 99kr, you'll get a Danish number plus about forty minutes of domestic calling time. The most commonly used network is TDC, but coverage with Telemore, Telenor and others is just as good. SIM cards and top-up credit can be bought in supermarkets, kiosks and phone shops.

Calling Denmark from abroad, the **international code** is ☎45. To make a **collect international call** from Denmark dial ☎80 30 40 00 – full instructions for this "Country Direct" system are displayed in phone booths (in English), and you can dial ☎80 60 40 50 for free assistance.

Post

The main post office is at Købmagergade 1 (Mon—Fri 10am—6pm, Sat 10am—2pm) and there's a late-opening one inside Central Station (Mon—Fri 8am—9pm, Sat & Sun 10am—4pm). Mail under 50g costs 12.50kr to other parts of Europe, and 14.50kr to the rest of the world. You can buy stamps from most newsagents and from post offices.

Smoking

Smoking is banned in all public buildings and restaurants. Bars and cafés under forty square metres which do not serve fresh food may still allow smoking. Many places have installed dedicated smoking booths but most prefer to smoke on the street.

Time

Denmark is one hour ahead of GMT, six hours ahead of US Eastern Standard Time, and nine ahead of US Pacific Standard Time.

Tipping

Service is included on all restaurant, hotel and taxi bills, so unless you feel you've been given exceptionally good service, tipping is not necessary.

Tourist information

The Copenhagen Visitor Centre (Mon—Fri 9am—4pm, Sat 9am—2pm; ☎70 22 24 42, ⌨visitcopenhagen.com), across the road from the Central Station at Vesterbrogade 4A, offers maps, general information and accommodation reservations, along with free accommodation-booking terminals.

Travellers with disabilities

Copenhagen is a model city for travellers with disabilities: wheelchair access, facilities and help are generally available at hotels, hostels, museums and public places. To see whether a place caters for travellers with disabilities, check the useful website ⌨godadgang .dk. Clicking the Good to know tab at ⌨visitcopenhagen.com brings up a list of attractions, hotels and restaurants with wheelchair access and information about disabled access to public transport.

Travelling with children

Copenhagen is a very child-friendly city with reserved children's pram areas on buses and trains, and children's menus and high seats available at most restaurants. The low level of traffic and many pedestrianized streets also make for a stress-free visit with kids. For more idea, see p.10.

Festivals and events

CPH:PIX

Eighteen-day film festival in April ⓦcphpix.dk
The city's premier film festival which features a wide range of Danish as well as classic international films in their original language. Most of the city's cinemas take part.

COPENHAGEN BEER FESTIVAL

Long weekend in May ⓦale.dk
A new and already very popular festival housed in the recently reopened TAP1 bottling hall in the Carlsberg area, featuring over a thousand different beers from around the world.

COPENHAGEN CARNIVAL

Whitsun weekend ⓦcopenhagencarnival.com
A mini Rio of samba and colourful costumes along Strøget and Købmagergade which culminates in all-night partying at Fælledparken supposedly allowing you to see the Whitsun sun "dance" as it rises in the early hours of the morning.

SANKT HANS AFTEN

Midsummer's eve ⓦvisitcopenhagen.com
Bonfires and traditional Danish folksongs at various locations along the Copenhagen coast. Check the tourist board website for locations and times.

ROSKILDE FESTIVAL

Last week of June or first week of July (see box p.111) ⓦroskilde-festival.dk
Four-day Glastonbury-style music festival in the outskirts of Roskilde preceded by four days' warm-up in the camping area.

COPENHAGEN JAZZ FESTIVAL

First or second week of July ⓦjazz.dk
Local and international jazz stars – young and old – take over the city's music stages and venues, as well many outside spaces, making it Europe's biggest jazz event. With loads of free gigs the entire city seems to be swinging to all sorts of jazz imaginable.

COPENHAGEN PRIDE

One week in July or August ⓦcopenhagenpride.dk
Superb week of gay events focused on the area around Frederiksholms Kanal and culminating in the flamboyant and colourful Gay Pride Parade which makes its way through the centre of town on the festival Saturday.

COPENHAGEN COOKING

Last week of August ⓦcopenhagencooking.dk
Riding on the Nordic cuisine popularity wave, over one hundred events across the city hosted by many of the city's famous chefs give you an opportunity the sample some of the amazing creations.

CHRISTMAS AND NEW YEAR'S

Leading up to Christmas – which is celebrated Christmas Eve – the city is aglow with festive lights and decorations, and *gløgg* and *æbleskiver* (a version of mulled wine and dough balls with apple inside) is sold everywhere. On New Year's Eve Rådhuspladsen is the scene of a massive fireworks fest, champagne drinking and kissing of strangers.

Chronology

1043 > The name "Havn" appears in the Knýtlinga Saga, described as the place Norwegian king Magnus sought cover after being defeated at sea.

1160 > Bishop Absalon is given control over "Havn" by his foster brother King Valdemar. Recent excavations have shown that Copenhagen at the time was a significant fishing village – Kongens Nytorv largely built on fish bones – and its residents unusually tall.

1167 > Bishop Absalon completes the construction of fortified Københavns Slot on current day's Slotholmen Island. Its aim is to protect the town's fishermen and traders from Wendish pirates.

1238 > The construction of the town's first monastery commences – today's Helligåndshus.

1249 > The earliest recorded attack and plunder of the town by a Hanseatic fleet from Lübeck.

1334 > With 5,000 inhabitants Copenhagen is Scandinavia's largest settlement.

1369 > The town is attacked and briefly occupied by Hanseatic forces who systematically dismantle Københavns Slot.

1417 > King Eric of Pomerania makes the newly reconstructed Københavns Slot his seat of power and residence of the royal family.

1443 > Copenhagen replaces Roskilde as Denmark's capital.

1479 > Copenhagen University, the first in Scandinavia, is established in today's Latin Quarter.

1536 > Protestant Reformation takes hold with the arrest of the Catholic Bishop of Copenhagen.

1588 > King Christian IV AKA "The Builder King" is born. After taking the throne at the age of ten he begins a life-long programme of works. Among his many feats are the neighbourhood of Christian-shavn, the city's defensive ring of moats, ramparts and Kastellet, Rosenborg Slot and Rundetårn.

1657 > Skåne is ceded to Sweden at the Treaty of Roskilde, Denmark's second most important town Malmö thereby becoming Swedish

1659 > After three years' siege, the city is stormed by Swedish troops.

1660 > Absolute monarchy is introduced.

1711 > Plague epidemic kills at least 22,000

1728 > The first "great fire" of Copenhagen destroys over a thousand buildings

1730 > King Christian VI decides to have Københavns Slot torn down and a much grander Louis XIV Rococo-style palace – renamed Christiansborg – is erected in its stead. It burns to the ground 28 years after its completion in 1766. Only the stables and riding ground survive.

1795 > The second great fire of Copenhagen burns Christiansborg to the ground.

1801 > British and Danish ships engage at the Battle of Copenhagen. Horatio Nelson famously turns a blind eye to Admiral Sir Hyde Parker's orders to retreat.

1807 > Fearing the Danes may side with Napoleon, the Royal Navy shells Copenhagen. After three nights of bombardment, large parts of the city lie in ruins. The Danish-Norwegian navy is surrendered to the British.

1828 > A new Romanesque style Christiansborg is completed

1836 > Hans Christian Andersen's *The Little Mermaid* is published

1838 > Sculptor Bertel Thorvaldsen returns to Copenhagen after forty years in Rome.

1843 > George Carstensen's brain-child Tivoli opens in the former rampart area.

1843 > Father of Existentialism Søren Kierkegaard's *Either/Or* is published.

1847 > J.C. Jacobsen founds the Carlsberg brewery just outside the city.

1884 > The second Christiansborg is burnt to the ground leaving only Christiansborgs Slotskirke standing.

1897 > The Ny Carlsberg Glyptotek is opened by philanthropic brewing magnate Carl Jacobsen, son of J.C.

1911 > The National Romantic Central Station stands completed.

1913 > The Little Mermaid statue by Edvard Eriksen (and paid for by Carl Jacobsen) is unveiled.

1928 > The current neo-Baroque Christiansborg is completed.

1940 > In the early hours of April 9, Copenhagen is occupied by German forces with barely a shot fired.

1943-1945 > Most of Denmark's Jewish population is smuggled successfully across to Sweden in fishing boats.

1971 > First Roskilde festival

1971 > Christiania is founded in disused military barracks on Christianshavn

1972 > Queen Margrethe II ascends the throne.

1973 > Denmark joins the EU.

1992 > The Danish football team wins the European Championship in a tense final against Germany. Millions line the streets to welcome them home.

2000 > The Øresunds link to Sweden is opened.

2005 > Crown Prince Frederik marries his Tasmanian bride Mary.

2007 > Detective Sarah Lund and her famous jumper first appear on Danish TV. Copenhagen-set *The Killing* soon becomes an international hit.

2010 > Copenhagen's *Noma* is rated as the world's best restaurant.

2011 > Construction begins on a new circular metro line, due to open 2018, and which will connect travellers to any corner of the city within thirty minutes.

Danish

In general, English is widely understood throughout Denmark, as is German, and young people especially often speak both fluently. However, even with little need to resort to Danish, learning a few phrases will surprise and delight any Danes you meet. If you can speak Swedish or Norwegian, then you should have little problem making yourself understood – all three languages share the same root.

There is no single word in the Danish language for "please". So when a Dane doesn't say "please" when speaking to you in English, it's not because they're rude – the word just doesn't come naturally. Danes are also renowned for being direct – if they want something they say "Give me..." – which can, incorrectly, be interpreted as impolite.

And idea of pronunciation is given in brackets below.

Basic words and phrases

Taler de engelsk? (tayla dee ENgellsg)	Do you speak English?
Ja (ya)	Yes
Nej (nye)	No
Jeg forstår det ikke (yai fus TO day igge)	I don't understand
Værså venlig (verso venli)	Please
Tak (tagg)	Thank you
Undskyld (unsgul)	Excuse me
Hi (hye)	Hello/Hi
Godmorgen (goMORN)	Good morning
Goddag (goDA)	Good afternoon
Godnat (goNAD)	Goodnight
Farvel (faVELL)	Goodbye
Hvor er? (voa ea?)	Where is?
Hvad koster det? (vath kosta day?)	How much does it cost?
Jeg vil gerne ha... (yai vay GERna ha)	I'd like...
Hvor er toiletterne ? (voa ea toaLETTaneh?)	Where are the toilets?
Et bord til ... (et boa te...)	A table for...
Må jeg bede om regningen? (moah yai beyde uhm RYningan?)	Can I have the bill/check, please?
Billet (billed)	Ticket

Food and drink basics

Bøfsandwich	Hamburger
Brød	Bread
Det kolde bord	Help-yourself cold buffet
Is	Ice cream
Ostebord	Cheese board
Peber	Pepper
Pølser	Frankfurters/sausages
Rugbrød	Rye bread
Salt	Salt
Sildebord	A selection of spiced and pickled herring
Kylling	Chicken
Oksekød	Beef
Svinekød	Pork
Kartofler	Potatoes
Fisk	Fish
Smør	Butter
Smørrebrød	Open sandwiches
Sukker	Sugar
Wienerbrød	"Danish" pastry
Øl	Beer
Fadøl	Draught beer
Guldøl	Strong beer
Vin	Wine
Husets vin	House wine
Hvidvin	White wine
Rødvin	Red wine
Mineralvand	Mineral water
Chokolade (varm)	Chocolate (hot)
Kærnemælk	Buttermilk
Kaffe (med fløde)	Coffee (with cream)
Mælk	Milk
Te	Tea
Vand	Water

PUBLISHING INFORMATION

This first edition published January 2014 by **Rough Guides Ltd**

80 Strand, London WC2R 0RL

11, Community Centre, Panchsheel Park, New Delhi 110017, India

Distributed by the Penguin Group

Penguin Books Ltd, 80 Strand, London WC2R 0RL

Penguin Group (USA) 345 Hudson Street, NY 10014, USA

Penguin Group (Australia) 250 Camberwell Road, Camberwell, Victoria 3124, Australia

Penguin Group (NZ) 67 Apollo Drive, Mairangi Bay, Auckland 1310, New Zealand

Penguin Group (South Africa) Block D, Rosebank Office Park, 181 Jan Smuts Avenue,
Parktown North, Gauteng, South Africa 2193

Rough Guides is represented in Canada by

Tourmaline Editions Inc., 662 King Street West, Suite 304, Toronto, Ontario, M5V 1M7

Typeset in Minion and Din to an original design by Henry Iles and Dan May.

Printed and bound in China

144pp includes index

A catalogue record for this book is available from the British Library

ISBN 978-1-40936-680-5

1 3 5 7 9 8 6 4 2

MIX
Paper from
responsible sources
FSC® C018179
FSC
www.fsc.org

ROUGH GUIDES CREDITS

Editors: Andy Turner and Edward Aves

Layout: Ankur Guha

Cartography: Katie Bennett and Ed Wright

Picture editor: Marta Bescos

Photographer: Diana Jarvis

Production: Charlotte Cade

Proofreader: Stewart Wild

Cover design: Wilf Matos

THE AUTHORS

Lone Mouritsen was born in Brazil to Danish parents and is co-author of the *Rough Guide to
Denmark*.

Roger Norum writes extensively on Scandinavia and is co-author of the *Rough Guide to Denmark*.

HELP US UPDATE

We've gone to a lot of effort to ensure that the first edition of **Pocket Rough Guide Copenhagen** is accurate and up-to-date. However, things change – places get "discovered", opening hours are notoriously fickle, restaurants and rooms raise prices or lower standards. If you feel we've got it wrong or left something out, we'd like to know, and if you can remember the address, the price, the hours, the phone number, so much the better.

Please send your comments with the subject line "**Pocket Rough Guide Copenhagen Update**" to ✉ mail@roughguides.com. We'll credit all contributions and send a copy of the next edition (or any other Rough Guide if you prefer) for the very best emails.

Find more travel information, connect with fellow travellers and book your trip on ⓦ roughguides.com

PHOTO CREDITS

All images © Rough Guides except the following:
(Key: a-above; b-below/bottom; c-centre; f-far; l-left; r-right; t-top)

p.1 copenhagenmediacenter.com/Ty Stange
p.4 Corbis/Ken Welsh/Design Pics
p.5 copenhagenmediacenter.com/Kasper Thye
p.8 copenhagenmediacenter.com/Columbus Leth (c)
p.9 Alamy/Peter Erik Forsberg/Lifestyle (b)
p.10 Alamy/Niels Quist (b)
pp.12–13 Corbis/Jean-Pierre Lescourret
p.14 Alamy/OJPHOTOS
p.15 Getty Images/Christian Kober (t); dreamstime.com/Jeewee (br)
p.17 Madklubben Steak (t); copenhagenmediacenter.com/Columbus Leth (cl); Noma/Ditte Isager (cr)
p.18 copenhagenmediacenter.com/Ty Stange
p.19 The Hirschsprung Collection (t); SuperStock/Photoservice Electa/Universal Images Group (b)
p.20 copenhagenmediacenter.com/Christian Alsing
p.21 copenhagenmediacenter.com/Christian Alsing (t & cr)
p.23 dreamstime.com/Tatiana Savvateeva (t); copenhagenmediacenter.com/Christian Alsing (cl & cr); Halvandet/uffekfoto.dk (b)
p.24 copenhagenmediacenter.com
p.25 copenhagenmediacenter.com/Tuala Hjarnø (cl). Mikkeller: (b)
p.27 Designmusem Danmark: (cr)
p.29 Getty Images/Robert Harding World Imagery/Marco Cristofori (t)
pp.30–31 dreamstime.com/Oleksiy Mark
p.32 copenhagenmediacenter.com/Ty Stange
p.34 copenhagenmediacenter.com/Ty Stange
p.35 Alamy/Heini Kettunen
p.36 copenhagenmediacenter.com/Ty Stange
p.38 dreamstime.com/Pixcom
p.40 Alamy/Claire Carrion
p.42 copenhagenmediacenter.com/Ty Stange (t)
p.43 copenhagenmediacenter.com/Tuala Hjarnø
p.46 Stilleben

p.47 copenhagenmediacenter.com/Christian Alsing
p.49 Royal Café
p.55 copenhagenmediacenter.com/Stine Avnbøl
p.56 The Danish Jewish Museum/Bitter + Bredt
p.58 dreamstime.com/Oleksiy Mark
p.60 dreamstime.com/Ferrari7a
p.61 Alamy: Robert Harding World Imagery
p.63 dreamstime.com/Krzysztof Janczewski
p.65 Grønbech & Churchill
p.66 copenhagenmediacenter.com/Admiral Hotel
p.67 Vespa
p.68 dreamstime.com/Ohmaymay
p.72 copenhagenmediacenter.com/Rasmus Flindt Pedersen
p.75 La Rocca
p.78 copenhagenmediacenter.com/Ty Stange
p.84 copenhagenmediacenter.com/Marie Louise Munkegaard
p.86 copenhagenmediacenter.com/Ty Stange
p.88 Alamy/Ken Welsh
p.89 copenhagenmediacenter.com/Christian Alsing
p.90 Alamy/Boginn Ljos
p.94 copenhagenmediacenter.com/Ty Stange
p.96 copenhagenmediacenter.com/Ty Stange
p.102 copenhagenmediacenter.com/Laundromat Cafe
p.103 copenhagenmediacenter.com/Christian Alsing
p.106 dreamstime.com/Valsador
p.108 copenhagenmediacenter.com/Poul Buchard
p.109 Dreamstime.com/Korshunova
p.110 Den Blå Planet
p.115 dreamstime.com/Mikhail Markovskiy
p.116 Bastard Malmö
p.117 Årstiderna by THE SEA
pp.118-119 copenhagenmediacenter.com/Miklos Szabo
pp.126-127 Corbis/Jean-Pierre Lescourret

Index

Maps are marked in **bold**.